Defensive Tactics from the Gangster Era

With commentary provided by members of the Rough And Tumble Society (RATS)

Robert H. Sabet

Defensive Tactics from the Gangster Era
Copyright © 2022 by Robert H. Sabet
Editor: Richard Bejtlich, Martial History Team

ISBN 978-1-387-66861-8

Dedication

To all the members of RATS. Thanks for the support.

Table of Contents

Foreword

How did this come to be? Robert Sabet, the main man, the driving force behind the Rough And Tumble Society Facebook page, suggested getting input from a variety of people on several 99-year old self-defense articles.

Are the techniques still valid? Do they need to be adapted to our modern times? Seven people volunteered to assess and analyze the techniques, offered by champion boxer Jack Dempsey and former US Marine Hand to Hand Fighting Instructor, Lieutenant K. E. Shepard.

The backgrounds of the participants are widely varied, with extensive knowledge of a variety of martial arts, from Japanese Jiu Jitsu and karate, to Filipino martial arts, WWII combatives, and more.

With such talents, the various insights and perspectives into the proffered techniques will prove interesting.

Cris Anderson
Combatives researcher and Jiu Jitsu black belt

Introduction

When I began hosting the Facebook group Rough And Tumble Society (RATS) I used to surf newspaper archives looking for interesting articles on self-defense tactics which I would clip and post in the group. Usually the articles I sought were from the 1940s, but I would often widen my search to other eras to see what else would turn up.

This was how I located the articles which would form the genesis of my second book on Ed Don George, who was a hand to hand combat instructor for the Navy during the second World War.

Jack Dempsey also made an appearance in that book. He was an unarmed combat instructor for the Coast Guard during the same period. Most people know he wrote some books on boxing and the unarmed combat manual *How To Fight Tough*. What most do not know is that he wrote a series of articles in 1923 on self-defense.

I presented those articles here. Interestingly enough during that same year another gentleman who was a defensive tactics instructor for the Long Beach police in Long Beach, California, also wrote a series of similar articles.

According to the articles, this gentleman, K. E. Shepard, had also been a hand-to-hand combat instructor for the Marines. Some of the tactics presented in the articles perhaps give an idea of what the Marines had been taught during the interwar period. One person who was responsible for the hand-to-hand combat and bayonet training of the Marines was Anthony Joseph Drexel Biddle. Biddle published *Do Or Die*, his book on hand-to-hand combat tactics, in 1937, and updated and republished it in 1944.

during the first World War, on June 8th, 1918, Biddle wrote a report for Marine Headquarters, titled *Notes on Bayonet Training.* In the report Biddle wrote the following concerning hand-to-hand combat tactics:

> At close quarters the fist should be used where the butt will reach. A right hand cross counter for the Jaw, backed by a rear foot advance will do the trick, and the opponent is stabbed when prostrate.

> Disarming is accomplished in various ways, principally by Jiu Jitsu holds. Pupils can use the method best suited to each, and they can invent methods.

> We learn from the French the art of the foot assault. It is a French art of attack known as La Savatte. In a clinch the knee is brought up with violence into the opponent's crotch or testicles. Or the foot is stamped on his instep. The most effective foot blow is delivered when bayonets are locked, when one of the two combatants stamps with his left foot on his adversary's upper shin bone, just below the knee. This dislocates or breaks the leg. These foot blows are all delivered with a stamp, as a boxer strikes with his full fist.

> A toe point kick throws the kicker off balance and must never be used. The forward stamp with the entire sole of the foot is more effective, and the equilibrium is maintained, hit or miss; with the stamp, the full power of the body backs up the blow, as in a boxer's straight arm punch. This Savatte system is unknown and unapplied in the otherwise most excellent British bayonet school.

> Unlike boxing, the eyes must not be watched. The bayonet must be the point of observation at all times. But the writer has

introduced boxing as the chief aid to bayonet instruction to obtain necessary coordination.

In an article about Biddle written by Robert Asprey for the Marine Corps Gazette, May 1967, titled *The King of the Kill*, Asprey wrote:

> A provisional captain at 43, Anthony Biddle was sent to Parris Island where for want of anything better, he was placed in charge of bayonet training. He took instantly to the weapon, swiftly mastered the prevalent drill and established his own physical fitness and bayonet training program.

Asprey continued:

> Transferred to Quantico in the autumn of 1917, Biddle continued his teachings. By now he realized the inadequacy of our bayonet drill and persuaded Headquarters, Marine Corps, to send him to Europe as an observer. He first visited a forward French division where, caught in a German raid, he was nearly captured. In training with the English he refused to wear protective gear and suffered a bad hand cut and finger break, the first of dozens. He next completed the bayonet course which the French were teaching the Americans at Gondrecourt, then returned to Paris to study the broadsword at the famed *Cercle Hoche* in an attempt to adapt this type of fighting to the bayonet. This experience led him to another type of fighter, a French detective who took him through the tough Apache quarter. As he later told his Marine students, "This fellow didn't carry any arms. All he needed was a piece of cord to subdue the toughest knife-wielding Apache." (Whereupon he effectively demonstrated the technique.)

> Captain Biddle returned to Quantico in the spring of 1918 greatly enriched by his observations. He was placed "in direct charge of

the instruction of all replacement units undergoing training for overseas duty... in bayonet fighting, physical training and recreational games." One of his students, Gene Tunney, recently informed the writer: "He was out early each morning putting the trainees through physical exercises. I remember him as though it were yesterday; he was in a gym shirt with a pair of long grey trousers and white shoes. Later in the day he gave us bayonet drill. He was absolutely fearless as far as his own life was concerned as he stood in front of any and all and brushed aside their bayonet thrusts."

Asprey continued:

Anthony Biddle's future service to his beloved Corps found expression in a number of ways. In the 25 years that followed World War I he gave of himself freely and unsparingly and in the process made himself one of the greatest hand-to-hand fighting experts in the world.

World War I had broadened the horizons previously confined to boxing. He did not lose interest in the sport. One of his first acts was to rejuvenate the ring in the stable behind his Walnut Street home. Here for years the boxing greats came, many of whom Biddle and his two sons, Livingston and Tony Jr., fought in serious matches. Here also came a generous sprinkling of reformed drunks, ex-convicts and other human beings who needed help.

Besides sparring with all the greats, Tony became a close friend with Tex Richard, the promoter; in 1919 he was a judge in Toledo where Dempsey won the title from Jess Willard. He also followed Gene Tunny's career very closely. At Stroudsburg, where Tunny was training for his first match against Dempsey in 1926, Maj

Biddle and Gen Lejeune showed up to give the young fighter a robe with the Marine Corps emblem on the back. Biddle later presided over the ceremony when Tunny was commissioned a first lieutenant in the Marine Corps Reserve. The following year, Maj and Mrs. Biddle were guests at the Speculator training camp before the second fight with Dempsey. Commander Tunney recently recalled: "There were boxers all over the place and he could not restrain himself from getting into the atmosphere. He boxed different sparring partners of mine during the training period and, on one occasion, he boxed for keeps. It seemed there was a barber in the camp who had been heavyweight boxing champion of Bulgaria. Maj Biddle took him on and almost ran him out of the ring; before the second round was over, the barber excused himself—he could take no more."

Was it possible that Biddle, with his outsized influence in the Marines as a bayonet and hand-to-hand combat expert, somehow influenced the Kenny Shepard from the articles?

The only information I found about Kenny Shepard was that there was a Kenneth E. Shepard serving as a second lieutenant in the Marines in 1919. Could that have been the same person? I was unable to find anything else. We have more questions than answers.

A series of articles in the Long Beach Telegram on self-defense are written by a Lieutenant K. E. Shephard, formerly an instructor in hand-to-hand fighting for the United States Marine Corps. We read very little about who he was other than he was a well-known expert. He doesn't turn up in any other newspaper articles from the period.

What was so special about the year 1923? For some of the answers I turned to the FBI website and found what I was looking for in the history section, in an article titled *The FBI and the American Gangster, 1924-1938.* It states:

> The 'war to end all wars' was over, but a new one was just beginning – on the streets of America.
>
> It wasn't much of a fight, really – at least at the start.
>
> On the one side was a rising tide of professional criminals, made richer and bolder by Prohibition, which had turned the nation "dry" in 1920. In one big city alone – Chicago – an estimated 1,300 gangs had spread like a deadly virus by the mid-1920s. There was no easy cure. With wallets bursting from bootlegging profits, gangs outfitted themselves with 'Tommy' guns and operated with impunity by paying off politicians and police alike. Rival gangs led by the powerful Al 'Scarface' Capone and the hot-headed George 'Bugs' Moran turned the city streets into a virtual war zone with their gangland clashes. By 1926, more than 12,000 murders were taking place every year across America.
>
> On the other side was law enforcement, which was outgunned (literally) and ill-prepared at this point in history to take on the surging national crime wave. Dealing with the bootlegging and speakeasies was challenging enough, but the "Roaring Twenties" also saw bank robbery, kidnapping, auto theft, gambling, and drug trafficking become increasingly common crimes. More often than not, local police forces were hobbled by the lack of modern tools and training. And their jurisdictions stopped abruptly at their borders.

People needed something to give them a feeling of confidence that they might be able to defeat the gangster. Knowing how to put a fugitive in a bear hug might be useful knowledge.

Shepard and Dempsey were trying to do their civic duty. They were trying to pass along some of the skills they had acquired in their careers so that the ordinary citizen and the law enforcement officer could go about their business and feel a sense of security.

Lieutenant K. E. Shepard

PRESENT LONG BEACH POLICE DEPARTMENT WITH 68 MEMBERS

Reading from left to right—Top row: Officer Ben Wood, Patrolman T. C. Wood, Patrolman J. Z. Helm, Patrolman A. R. Munson, Patrolman M. B. Payne, Patrolman Robert L. Wright, Patrolman Robert Houghton of the traffic squad, Patrolman M. M. Richardson of the purity squad, Acting Patrol Sergeant J. P. Davison, Patrolman Harry Scott, Patrolman William Sims, Patrolman L. P. Gott; Patrolman Jack Moran of the "booze" squad, Acting Patrol Sergeant W. J. Ray, Patrolman C. O. Bizant, Patrolman Claude Reusch, Patrolman Joe Hale of the traffic squad, Patrolman Earl B. Porter, Patrolman J. B. Worley of the bogus check squad, Patrolman O. E. Bridgeman, Patrolman George McConahay, Patrolman W. F. Hackers and Patrolman W. A. Maganety.

Center row: Motorcycle Officer George Manners, Mounted Officer "Bill" Brown, Patrolman Malcom Kirkpatrick, Patrolman O. M. Murphy, Patrolman Alva Davis, Patrolman J. E. Daly, Patrolman George Brown of the traffic squad, Bailiff William G. Wingfield, Mounted Officer George Loper, Patrolman Alonzo White, Patrolman R. C. Miller, Patrolman Joseph Wofford, Patrolman F. G. Henderson, Patrolman H. E. LeBarron, Patrolman R. E. Moore, Patrolman Sam Bailey, Patrolman A. H. Smith of the "booze" squad, Patrolman Jack Panner of the traffic squad, Patrolman George Barry of the traffic squad, Patrolman Barney Kane of the purity squad, Patrolman J. D. Taylor, Patrolman R. B. Fridley.

Bottom row: Patrolman J. J. Delaney, Special Officer G. Campbell, Special Officer F. L. Brown, Special Officer H. H. Dunn, Special Officer J. F. Chubbic, Special Officer C. S. Wingfield, Patrolman George McCrindle, garage mechanic; Patrolman Lloyd Christensen, identification clerk; Matron Laura Fleming, Policewoman Lulu Straw, Matron Edna Raysome, Police Surgeon F. D. Sweet, Police Chief Ben W. McLendon, Sergeant J. B. Yancy, Sergeant Gershon A. Llewellyn, Sergeant Clyde Allen, Sergeant William Dovey, Superintendent F. B. Kutz, Captain O. C. Mitchell, Detective Ralf Alyea, Detective C. F. Robberson, Detective T. G. Cervantes.

Returning to K. E. Shepard, I was able to locate an article which contained a photograph of the Long Beach police department dated May 7th 1922. hat photo did not depict him nor did it contain any description of him.

The first mention of Shepard appears in an article in the Long Beach Telegram, October 17th 1923, titled *Telegram Readers to Have Opportunity to Learn Self Defense Thru New Feature.*

It stated:

> Men and women, boys and girls, here's an unusual opportunity to learn the art of self-defense.

> Beginning next Sunday, The Telegram will publish an illustrated series of articles on "Self Defense," by Lieut. K. E. Shepard, an expert, who will describe in detail various ways of resisting a holdup man or other assailant. Long Beach police officers praise this feature highly.

If every citizen would learn to master some form of self-defense, holdups and assaults in Long Beach could be reduced to a minimum.

That is the opinion of Chief of Police J. S. Yancy.

"I am glad that the Telegram is planning the series of 'Self Defense,' by Lieut. K. E. Shepard," the chief declared, "and if The Telegram's readers will study the lessons presented I believe they will benefit greatly.

"Especially do I believe women should absorb the lessons taught in 'Self Defense." We are not troubled to any great extent with mashers. Nevertheless, were all women to master the art of self-defense these curbstone, sheiks would be eliminated, for they are not going to accost the women who displays ability to protect herself.

"If a man would master this art he would be in a position to successfully cope with any holdup man. The thug labors under the impression that the average citizen, when commanded to 'put 'em up,' does so from sheer fright. He depends entirely upon frightening his intended victim to accomplish his ends.

"The man who has mastered the art of self-defense is never frightened. In fact, he is as cool as the thug. And, that adds greatly to his advantage.

"By all means, I say, let every citizen read 'Self Defense." Not only read it, but study it, and practice it."

"Self Defense" starts in the Telegram next Sunday, October 21. There will be one article daily, each illustrated with a drawing showing a different method of resisting or overpowering an assailant.

Don't miss any of the series. Each article will be of interest, and knowledge gained from any one of them may prove at some time or other to be of great value.

In the same newspaper the next day the Captain of Detectives chimed in:

"Mastering the art of self-defense never did anyone any harm and, of course, for many it has proved tremendously valuable."

So said Captain of Detectives Jack B. Worley today, anent the announcement yesterday that The Telegram will publish a series of 18 illustrated articles, beginning next Saturday, on the subject of "Self Defense," prepared by Lieut. K. E. Shepard, a well-known expert.

"Everyone should study these lessons," Captain Worley continued, "and practice the grips and movements.

"Maybe you never will have actual occasion to use it, but knowing it will certainly do you no harm.

"You may master self-defense, and go months without having to practice it. Then suddenly you may be accosted by a thug or, if you are a woman, by a masher. Knowing this art, you certainly have an advantage over the person who doesn't know it.

"There are times, perhaps when stopped by a highwayman that one is not given an opportunity to successfully combat the thug. But, the majority of times, you, knowing the principals of 'Self Defense,' are successfully able to cope with him. Many times, not only saving your money, but placing the thug behind the bars where he belongs.

"Yes, I feel that I am offering good advice when I urge everyone to master these lessons which are scheduled to run in The Telegram. And I believe you will be surprised to learn how rapidly you will become adept at the practice."

The two commentators appearedin the picture from 1922. On October 19th the Captain of Police said:

"No matter in what walk of life a man is engaged he is very apt to find at some time or another that a knowledge of self-defense is useful."

That declaration was made today by Captain of Police Claude Robberson when he heard that The Telegram is planning to publish a series of lessons in "Self-Defense" by Lieutenant K. E. Shepard, beginning next Sunday, October 21.

"There never was anyone, man, woman or child, who ever lost anything by possessing a knowledge of self-defense. Certainly I advise everyone to master these lessons. What I have seen of them are good," said Captain Robberson.

"Patrolmen and those who guard lives and property should, by all means, master the art of self-defense. To them it is essential. In fact. It is essential to anyone who is out on the streets at night.

"Men are quicker to learn these things than women, but I certainly recommend that every woman in the city absorb these lessons. It will be a great step toward ridding Long Beach of mashers who accost women. Under present conditions there is nothing a woman can do except ignore these advances. If she would master self-defense she could guard the man until an officer could arrive to arrest him.

"By all means, I say, let everyone learn these lessons and if occasion ever arises put that knowledge into practice."

Finally on Saturday, October 20th Detective Sergeant Ralf Alyea, can be seen in the photo, added:

Recommending that everyone make special efforts to become proficient to some degree in the art of self-defense, Detective Sergeant Ralf Alyea of the Long Beach police department today lauded The Telegram's publication of the series of illustrated articles by Lieutenant K.E. Shepard. The series will begin in tomorrow morning's Telegram and one article will appear daily, each accompanied by a drawing.

"If everyone would master such lessons as these, many an attempted holdup or other attack would be frustrated," said Detective Sergeant Alyea.

"Of course, there are many times when a highwayman gets there are numerous times when the victim could easily frustrate the plans of the robber. A knowledge of self-defense aids the victim to remain cool. When cool, naturally he can think quicker and clearer. He sees openings which he would not otherwise see. Self-defense is seeing an opening and knowing in an instant what to do.

"Yes," everyone should read these lessons; not only read them, but absorb and practice them until able to use them perfectly.

When this is done, successful holdups will be reduced to a minimum, and I believe more thugs will land in jail."

I thought it would be interesting to invite some of the members of the group I am a part of, The Rough And Tumble Society (RATS), to provide commentary on the techniques that were presented by Lieutenant Shepard and later on by Jack Dempsey.

The people who have provided commentary are either practitioners of different martial arts or combatives systems, or they are instructors of those systems. I wanted to offer the reader some insight into how these techniques are perceived today and whether or not they have stood the test of time. The commenters show what they like or dislike about the technique, and perhaps what could be done better.

The following individuals have provided commentary:

Cris Anderson
Michel Dé
Chris Hennessey
Barry Drennan
Tommy Joe Moore
Mike Smith
Jerry Powell

The material presented in the following chapters has been taken from a series of articles titled 'Self-Defense' which were written by Lieutenant K.E. Shepard for the Long Beach Telegram in October 1923.

Starting on page 88, a series of articles titled "How to Repel a Thug" are also presented. They were written by Jack Dempsey for the Buffalo Courier in March 1923.

Breaking the Wrist Grip

NO. 1. BREAKING THE WRIST GRIP

This is the first of a series of illustrated lessons in the interest of "Self-Defense." This lesson and those which follow contain only the fundamental information which will at some time or other prove useful to every man, woman and child who studies them.

Master the simple tactics presented each day by working out each lesson with a partner. Apply the holds with the idea of learning to develop speed

21

and accuracy and in practicing do not apply any of them too forcefully nor try to resist them.

As the effectiveness of the different holds depends largely on the element of surprise, it is necessary that you learn to apply them rapidly.

Learn the principle. Be sure that the instructions are followed to the exact detail, for the slighting of any movement may make the action ineffective. With the knowledge of these holds you will be able to take care of yourself in almost any situation.

In a hand to hand encounter strong men often seize the weaker by the wrist in a vise-like grip. This grasp can easily be broken without very much effort.

Jerk the arm sharply in a direction which will carry it thru the assailant's finger tips and the tip of his thumb, twisting the wrist at the same time. The thumb and tips of the fingers are not strong enough to maintain the hold. The strongest grip is ineffectual at the end of the thumb. Remember that it is the combination of the jerk and the twisting motion that does the business.

Bob: Basic technique. Learned this one in judo a long time ago. You have the other hand free here too so can always bring that into the fight. Chop him right in the neck or punch him in the throat.

It's kind of interesting to see the range of techniques from almost like "why bother?" to blitzkrieg type attacks. Also these are only mainly dealing with one person attacker scenarios. Usually that's always the case with these instructional articles from back in the day but often that's not how it actually goes down on the streets. You can easily find yourself in situations where there are more than one assailant.
Anyway regarding this particular technique, Fairbairn even has them in his so it appears to be something which is taught quite often. Is this considered a core technique?

Cris: Work the path of least resistance. Easier to break the grip working against the thumb than going against the palm and four fingers.

A hammerfist to the face is a good follow-up to enable a quick exit.

Barry: In my experience, this a very functional way of breaking a single-handed-wrist-grip.

This specific version, along with the two-handed-version, even made it into the eleven release-techniques in Get Tough.

I have encountered several variations of this. In all cases, the core mechanics remain. In fact, over time I have tested this release hundreds of times. Tested against an entire spectrum of possible applicants, it rarely fails.

Having given the method a positive score for functionality; I now look to scoring it for practical usability.

I clearly see this as a passive counter to a questionable scenario. A victim can quickly deduce whether the wrist-grab is part of an immediate threat or an intolerable inconvenience. As a response to an inconvenience, it has my support as a go-to.

However, as an answer to threat, it falls short in that it gains an escape at the cost of alerting the aggressor to the potential of greater resistance while simultaneously setting him free, unharmed and fully capable of reinitiating his attack.

For the latter case I would advocate avoiding this technique in favor for making a decisive strike designed to create shock or injury. Situation demanding, alternative options are determined by circumstance, and numerous in quantity.

Chris: Yeah, this is basic. I've taught this as well as the 2 hand version (clasp your hands together and then pull to release). Gotta make sure you follow up with something though…

Jerry: This is good for a non-violent bully attack. Add the yell No! Or Stop!! To distract or draw attention to yourself.

If a violent controlling attack : if you cannot run then yell and jerk out wrist at attacker's forefinger and thumb area or opening, repeat jerk as needed then with the same hand strike with a side of hand blow to the neck as needed.

Tommy:

To be honest, I have very little faith in techniques like this. Whilst' 'monster sized man'. I'm 6ft 2 and a heavyweight. No way on earth is someone's wrist coming out of my hand early.

And let's be frank, the technique in real life (if not a prelude to a strike), will be done whilst moving. Breaking a grip whilst being ragged and dragged around is much more difficult.

I'd only use this technique to showcase the 'exit point' of a grip.

But that is more of a principle, as a 'technique' or a counter to violence, much more is needed such as keeping your balance, attacking points like the eyes, and understanding you may need your second arm to break the first free.

Wrist Break – Disarming a Knife Hand

No. 2. Wrist Break —Disarming a Knife Hand

The successful application of this simple but very effective defensive strategy depends upon the quickness of your action as well as your coolness "under fire," but the most dangerous assailant wielding a knife with murderous intent, can be quickly and easily subdued by a person far inferior in physical strength.

Seize the attacker's knife arm just below the wrist and apply the open palm of the left hand vigorously against his closed knuckles

The knife hand will immediately fly open under pressure, and by bearing down hard you will break his wrist.

The effectiveness of this action can be readily seen by trying it out with a friend, but be careful not to exert too much pressure in practice.

Jerry: Good for a non-violent bully attack. Add the yell "No!!! Stop!!!" If violent jerk and run, if cannot run then yell, jerk, release, repeated same hand side hand to neck at opportune time, check trap arms (hard if big person). Knee strike to the groin.

Knife: Never done or practiced this. Seems like you would have to side step, off line, and react with stress-speed-surprise or it would be hard to catch/trap the attacker's hand.

Bob: I have to admit I've been saving commentary on the knife encounter ones for last because knives are a really tense subject. There is knife crime all over NYC at the moment. I know what someone I know from RATS would say on this one – you can trap the attacker's one hand with the knife but he still has the other one free…Usually the technique utilized for defense of the underhand knife attacks is different than this one in the article. This one the way it's done in the article it seems destined to fail.

Side-stepping is a definitely a great technique though. It's something that I was taught to do.

Someone rushes at you with a knife side-step quickly to the side to avoid the thing coming at you. I recall that the person who taught it to me said it's a technique that comes from Bruce Tegner.

With knife stuff I think of a line from a movie I saw. Al Pacino's character says "You charge a guy, always charge a guy with a gun. With a knife, you run away. Run away from the knife. So you can charge with a gun, with a knife, you run."

Barry: Complete garbage in my opinion. Firstly, there are multiple points that dispel this method as viable. Secondly, there is a host of better options to choose from.

To start by admitting prejudice; I am not big believer in the snapping weapons out of people's hands thing. In the same line-of-thought, nor do I accept that the grabbing of wrists is immune to missing, avoidance, slippage, poor grip, and reactive or responsive counters. Further there are extremely dangerous speed and accuracy-tradeoffs.

In addition, it is logical to accept that when an opponent's brain remains totally functional, disarms are susceptible to problems evolving from traversing range, grip acquisition, position/angle of the assailant's arm during the duration of achieving control (i.e. breaking the wrist grip), and whether the knife is held in a death-grip or not.

As for the physiology of grasping the wrist of the knife hand; pressure applied to the inside surface of the wrist actions a closure of the fingers. This closing-effect is further increased by bending the hand inwards towards the inside-of-the-forearm.

Moving from physiology to physics; the moment upon a force strikes a hinged surface and breaks inertia that surface begins to move away from the applied-force. As the surface folds away from the applied-force, the ever-increasing angle of the surface creates an ever-decreasing applied-force. E.g. 10lbs applied at 90 degrees to a flat surface delivers 10lbs of applied-force, but at 45 degrees the same 010lbs delivers only 5lbs of applied-force. These hardly support a release of the weapon.

Cris: Disarming a knife is always risky, but violently forcing a wrist to bend beyond its normal range of motion will force the fingers open, dropping the knife.

I would suggest slamming the knife bearing hand with a palm heel, rather than placing your hand on his knuckles and trying to force the hand to bend.

Chris: I think I would only grab like this if I hit the guy first and he was stunned for a second or two. Just catching a downward stab like this is risky at best. As far as striking the hand, yeah, I would smack the hell out of it with a palm strike or well-placed punch with knuckles to the top of the hand.

Tommy:

Nooooooo way in hell would I risk my life on this one. Ice Pick attacks are nearly always done with forward pressure and murderous intent. Hammer grips are often used in threat – if someone want you dead, they often use the ice-pick method.

There's also very little merit for using the palm vs the knuckles. Punching the assailants hand will at least cause more damage and more pain. But even then, I feel this technique is more for the stage than the street.

There are plethora of alternatives out there, but universal good sense is always:

        a) get out the way
        b) if you can't jam the attack
        c) wrap it up with two arms on one and
        d) beat the bejesus out of the chap.

The Pistol Arm Break

No. 3. The Pistol Arm Break

The first action in defense against a pistol attack should be toward getting the pistol hand in a harmless position.

As your assailant reaches for his pistol, seize his right (pistol arm) wrist with your left hand and force this arm sharply upward keeping his wrist and pistol pointed down simultaneously, with your right hand, grasp his right arm above the elbow (see illustration.)

With your left hand force his wrist to the rear, and at the same time jerk his elbow to the front.

This movement, applied quickly and vigorously may dislocate his shoulder, or will at least cause pain enough to make him drop his pistol and give you the advantage in the encounter. Follow the illustration carefully.

In case he has already drawn his pistol and has you "covered." I would not advise resistance unless he actually intends to shoot.

Bob: This technique reminds me of something Chris taught me once. Looking for the V. I never practiced it more than the one time he showed me the technique but if the person is reaching in their pocket for a knife for example, their elbow would bend and you would spot that and put a stop to them before they take the thing out. Look for the V.

Jerry: Seems to me the wrist arm/wrist grabs need to be sudden quick unexpected and are difficult on a big boned or muscled up person. Quick and unexpected or otherwise forget it. Start running.

Barry: Although I much like the preemptive nature of this technique, as it alludes to situational-awareness and knowing what is going on around you. Another good-point is that when executed in this manner, the joints lock-up exceptionally quick.

I would note that it is are several speed and accuracy-tradeoffs. Most methods where the brain is not affected remain susceptible to variations evolving from traversing range, grip acquisition, angle of the assailant's forearm during the duration of achieving control, angular range of wrist-movement of the gun-hand itself, and the requirement [*situation depending] to get off-line; all with particular attention to a reactive or responsive firing of the gun.

If the disarm degenerates into a wrestling-match over weapon-control, a jujitsu person or a wrestler would have immediate follow-ups to aid them. A person with limited repertoire on the other hand would be well advised to have a specific plan-B in reserve.

Like many of the gun-disarms, this technique is susceptible to the assailant countering the disarm by simply dropping to a knee or, falling down and rearward. In either case, the maneuver is accompanied by a simultaneous firing of the gun.

At this point I recall the words of German GSG9 fellow I trained with; "The best part about weapons disarming is that you only do it when you think you are going to die. In which case you can do whatever you want, … because you are already dead.".

Tommy:

Doable if you have surprise on your side before they draw. Would it be my go-to? Unlikely.

More attention needs to be paid to getting yourself off the firing line, or getting that pistol away from you and offline.

But credit, where credit's due – it's good to see a proactive approach to attacking the man drawing the pistol before he can get it on target.

Cris: Fouling the draw of a weapon, whether a gun, a knife or a blunt object is imperative to stopping a bad situation from becoming worse. Recognizing the action that must be taken to draw a weapon into action is a vital skill.

31

Once you have your hands on his wrist and upper arm, you could quickly transition to a hammer lock.

Chris: I actually teach something like this… you have to be aware of the position of the hand though (the "shooter's triangle" or the V as was mentioned earlier). Being able to recognize it and react when you do comes with training. It also comes with hitting. Clasp and hit, clasp and kick. You have to do something to stun or stop the attacker.

Breaking the Throat Hold

NO. 4. BREAKING THE THROAT HOLD

This defense will be of particular interest to women. There is no need to fear the terrible strangling grip from an assailant's powerful fingers. Notice how ridiculously simple it is to break such a hold.

When your assailant grasps you by the throat, throw your arms, hands upward, close to your body and between the arms of your assailant. Then fling them apart sharply. The strongest grip is thus easily thrown aside, for no matter how powerful the fingers of your assailant may be they cannot withstand the sudden blow from your own upper arm as it is brought sideways and downward.

Bob: Basic technique learned in judo. I also recall a friend who taught me WW2 Combatives telling me in a lesson once that this might not necessarily work, for example what if the guy has beefy arms?

Well if the thugs arms are tied up like that you could attempt to do a double ear smash followed up by an eye gouge. I think that's what he told said. Only problem with that, is if the opponent has longer arms.

I have seen other methods for getting out of this jam too but this is a basic one I was taught way back when.

Cris: Raise one hand up high (Teacher! Teacher!), it will lift your shoulder, relieving some pressure on your throat.

Turn out and drop raised arm across both arms.

Follow with the edge of hand blow. Or sidestep to the right and hammerfist the ribs with your left, or sidestep and kick the knee (Tegner kick).

Jerry: Works as a release if it's a non-violent bully intimidation attack.

If oncoming, step one foot back for stability, break attacker's arm to side and or down to possible head grab with thumbs in eyes or a knee strike.

Chris: Just hit the guy. Don't waste time with all of this. With his hands on you, and your hands free, its anything goes. Just hit the guy. Uppercut, chin jab, knee, whatever. Just hit the guy.

Tommy:

Can work if there is parity in weight/strength. But not advised. This tends to only happen against something (the wall, the floor). In open space, just punch them, attack the eye and move back as you do so. Attention should be paid when the neck is gripped to dropping the chin and raising shoulders to keep what air supply (and blood) that you can.

Two free hands can cause a lot more damage to the eyes and throat of the attacker. And rightly so. Any attack on your neck, is an attack on your life.

Barry: Here, refer to my reply to my review of "No. 5 Breaking the Throat Hold and Countering."

Breaking the Throat Hold and Countering

NO. 5. BREAKING THE THROAT HOLD AND COUNTERING

The breaking of a throat, or strangle hold, as illustrated, is so ridiculously simple that one wonders why the idea had never occurred to him before.

When seized about the throat, clasp your hands tightly in front of your body. Move them sharply in a vertical circle from left to right and no assailant can maintain his grip against the force of your arms. In fact, he will be thrown off his balance, and your own position will be such that you can retaliate quickly with a knockout punch to the jaw with your right fist.

Bob: I was shown a very simple way to repel this type of attack. You jab your fingers into the jugular notch and push down. It causes a gag reflex type response which then causes them to release their hands.

I've probably seen this version in the article demonstrated before or some variation of it.

Cris: I think a cleaner version than windmilling clasped hands would be cross cut and swing. Grab his right hand with your left, raise right hand high and drop down on both arms while turning out.

If you hang onto his right hand, you have options. Wrist lock takedown if you're so inclined. Smash your forearm against his forearm, disrupting his balance further while taking additional step(s) back to take him to the ground.

Mike: That's my preferred option too for this one, while I would add to the description to turn to your right to assist in breaking the hold.

Chris: Again, just hit the guy. See above.

Barry: I view everything through the lens of "high-effectivity, more-for-less, reduced-repertoires". This puts me at odds with this technique.

Functionally and the biomechanical susceptibility and leverage advantages are solid. The results being the defender having their arm over and somewhat controlling the aggressor's arm is strong. Therefore, this response offers sound opportunities in terms of gaining momentary-control and counter-attacking.

37

In adding that the technique is very functional for both the competent combatant as well as the person of smaller stature, I rate this technique as strong. Having given the method a strong positive score for functionality; In terms of usability, I give it a poor rating.

In recognition, any strangle holds a lethal potential. Suffocation is quick to achieve, quick in negating an effective response because the victim's reactive-window is counted in single digit seconds. A choke's debilitating effects remain after the escape has been successful. From my personal experience, resulting from ripping a strong or trained grip off the trachea is valid secondary risk of injury. In such cases gaining a good gasp of air can also be compromised.

My prejudice would go to more decisive responses. Speed is of the essence. Trade-offs are few. Alternate responses would hinge-off our reflexive flinch reaction of grasping the assailant's wrists. From there rotating the shoulders while retaining this grip [on one or both wrists depending], allows the free-hand to viciously finger(s)/thumb jab into the assailant's eyes or v-notch. Another option would be using low-line-kicking, stomps, or shin-scrapes to attack the lower-legs.

The minimum result from either of these attacks would be the gaining a good gasp of air. The maximum outcome would be a strong reversal of advantage.

Tommy:

I have two free hands to hit with. Why would I lock them both together? This would only work if you're as strong, or stronger than the adversary.

However, it's violent lateral movement as suggested is a good move. But better accompanied by striking and dipping the chin / raising the shoulder for safety. And few of these techniques mention balance. People often

MOVE when doing this. Staying on your feet as you're ragged about by the neck is vital.

Mike: So I tried this one in my class on Tuesday, and while it did work in breaking the hold, my partner was able to recover very quickly while my arms were 'out of action' due to spinning them around. I class this one as 'works, but circumstantial'.

Breaking the Body Squeeze

NO. 6. BREAKING THE BODY-SPUEEZE

A common assailant is one who, relying upon his superior strength, rushes
in and embraces his victim with a "bear" hug, which forces the breath from

the victim's lungs. Men and women are safe from this attack if they remember this counter.

Hold your arms close to your body, making your assailant pin your arms to your sides. Clench your fists tightly and bring them together in front of the abdomen. When he starts to squeeze, jab your fists viciously into his body just below the ribs. He cannot stand this treatment. Keep your fists in place and he will give up the idea. Try it out. It's effectiveness will surprise you.

Jerry: Have used this for non-violent bully releases if striking with fist, strike upward 45 degree angle, short snapping strike repeatedly shock the liver. Also have used hammer strikes and side of hand. Always be ready for the attacker to escalate the attack.

Bob: Good when you are on the ground too. Attack the ribs, good place to attack if they are exposed.

Barry: I can't support this technique as described.

My immediate reflection upon the first step of "holding my arms by my body" is that this maneuver is ludicrous. In the situation described, if I had half a second and a moment of thought, there would be a host of other better options that could be brought into play. Spin the lens to where I don't have the luxury of time or thought, then time-restriction would preclude my ability to pre-position my arms.

It has been my experience with frontal arms held bear-hugs that they are rammed-in, off-balancing, seizures that pit brute strength against brute strength. As such, upper-arm movement of any kind is a battle of strength against strength where the aggressor has already seized the advantage via the element-of-surprise, size, mass, balance, muscular strength, and method of locking their arms together [* hand locked over wrist for example],

41

and lifting of the victim. Immobilized from shoulder to elbow, power generation from the forearms and hands is minimal at best.

Given choice of arm-position, having the victim's hands closer to the assailant's privates would enable the victim to protect their own while simultaneously attacking the assailant. From this proximity, the victim could inflict injurious grips and twists to the assailant's testicles which could create opportunity and potentially avoid being lifted.

The differences in height, body form, fat vs thin vs muscular, state-of mind [* adrenalized vs rage vs drunk vs doped], can be such that medium to low power "short-shot" pressures or impacts to the liver or spleen areas [*ideally] can produce wildly unreliable results. (*Having once while boxing "fought through" a "liver-punch" that was substantial enough to show "liver-repair-enzymes" in a subsequent blood-test I can personally attest to this point).

Even if "keeping my fists in place" did result in my assailant "giving-up"; I would still prefer to attempt something more aggressive. Something that offers greater gains.

Given upper-body proximity, I would butt or bite or both. Given leg-movement, low-kicks, shin-scrapes and instep-stomps would be my attempt. All of these offer secondary options better than an unpredictable "giving-up".

Chris: Yeah, I can see how this can work. Of course, if you can't get your hands in the right spot due to being squeezed too hard, you won't be able to do it.

Tommy:

It may buy you time, but spend that time well. Soon as you've survived the initial "crush" you'd be well advised to start working for a decent underhook and then freeing one hand as you drop your weight.

With an underhook and a free hand, you have great options for striking or throwing. But sure, as a way to survive an immediate two hand over bear hug, there's worse out there. But only for the initial crush.

Cris: Double punches up into the floating ribs will definitely take the air out of most men, allowing you an opportunity to quickly counter. A backfist to the groin, a grab and squeeze of the groin (monkey steals the peach), a shin kick or knee to the groin are all suitable follow-ups.

Another Counter for the Body Squeeze

NO. 7. ANOTHER COUNTER FOR THE BODY SQUEEZE

In the last lesson we assumed that you were quick enough to keep your assailant from slipping his arms inside of yours when he was attempting to grasp you about the body. If he has attained his grip before you get your arms on the inside, there is still another counter for you to use but its success depends entirely upon your own quickness of action.

The instant you realize that his arms slipping inside of yours and next to your body, clasp your hands vigorously in front of your body and pin his elbows together. The whole strength of your arms against his elbows will be effective. He will not be able to close his hands about you.

Bob: I don't know about this one... It speculates that you would be able to frustrate the guy's attack as he is about to bear hug you by locking his elbows in. If some guy is rushing at you and you have any time to react hit him with a tiger claw or a chin jab or a swivel punch, etc. etc. Why lock him up and hold him close? He's just going to bite that ear off.

Barry: I am often boggled by what people see as self-defense. Here I see this prescribed solution as nothing less than ludicrous. I really shake my head as this method basically takes the defender nowhere.

In this technique, the defender is first instructed to respond to an aggressor's attempt to gain a bear-hug by lowering your guard [exposing their head] and squeezing his elbows together.

If there was a substantial chance to hyper-extend the aggressor's elbows to a point of disabling their arms, there could be some value. However, this seems unlikely as disabling requires pressure to be applied into the "point-of-the-elbow" side of the elbow joint. First you have to gain a relatively precise arm to elbow-joint position, and the space between defender and aggressor required to enable the hyper-extension.

Generally frontal-bear-hugs by habit tend to be a chest-to-chest power-driven constriction. Such applications rarely offer a usable space between them.

Any other usable success is hard to determine as compressing the assailant's arms when their elbows point to the ground only achieves a lock. Once a lock offers no destruction, then it only offers an equalized race to who responds first, e.g. who head-butts, bites, low kicks, shin-scrapes, etc., first.

There are just too many options to make this one a "go-to".

Jerry: A goofing off technique. Playing around.

Cris: Not a fan of this technique. While you have managed to trap both his arms, you have also locked up both your arms, making a counter technique more difficult. It is possible to twist to the side to off balance him, but that will be size dependent.

As the person is grabbing you under the arms, attacking the head with slaps, punches, elbows or head butts makes more sense to me. Knee strikes to the groin are another possibility.

Michel:
I was taught to apply this one above the elbow joints, squeeze and lift my arms, thereby hyperextending the opponent's elbows. Most of the time the opponent just blasted forward through your attempt to lock them up.

This then opened them up to all kinds of more efficient counters as your hands were free. You could also head butt or knee him in the groin, however he could do the same to you when you try to execute this technique.

Chris: NO! Just knee the guy in the balls and call it a day.

Mike: I am surprised by this one and don't see why it would be worth publishing when the author already states that it is hard to execute. Stick with the simple techniques that work.

46

The aggressor would have to be really half arsed at attacking to time this one well, and any attempt would be easily countered. Without trying to physically see what would work against someone pressing your elbows together, the first that comes to mind would be to angle the shoulders and extend one arm under the defender's armpit and close in, bringing that arm over their shoulder thus locking it. That is just one that comes to mind, either way I feel like the defender has dropped their guard, committed too much to a weak defence and leaving themselves totally vulnerable.

Tommy:

If you nail the timing, possible. But you need strong, long arms. I can pull this technique off well because I have those attributes. But the ideal range for this is so fleeting, as it cannot be achieved once body to body, nor can it be achieved too early before the hands clasp. If those hand are free, put them to use and take an eyeball, crush a larynx, or elbow the jaw. No need for faff.

Shoulder and Knife Break

NO. 8. SHOULDER AND KNIFE BREAK

This is a dramatic action, combining defense with attack. Moving picture heroes often apply variations of this hold in their hand to hand combats. Your assailant, with a knife in his right hand, is grasped by his right wrist, by your left hand. Your first action is to pull the knife arm past you to a harmless position. Retaining your grasp on his wrist, strike your opponent heavily with the flat of your forearm at his collar bone. This action will throw him backward, and if you have inserted your heel behind his right leg, he will fall heavily on his back and be at your mercy.

This action may appear to be complex, but in reality is quite simple and with practice can be performed like a flash. You are really doing three things almost simultaneously; jerking his wrist behind you, striking him sharply on the collar bone, and tripping him. Practice this a few times and see how quickly and efficiently it works.

Bob: This one reminds me of something I learned from training with Chris. I think the technique he was demonstrating comes from Krav but it's the same idea. You try to tie up the attacking knife hand and keep it close to the body.

He showed it being done with a chin jab but this attack of the collarbone might do the trick as well and get the person to drop the knife. Could do a hammer fist to the solar plexus too. There are options but I guess the general idea is to tie up the hand with the knife.

Good luck with that in reality but maybe against some clown who has no knife fighting skills and is high or drunk...

Barry: In analyzing this technique, I am most concerned with how the wrist of the knife-hand is grabbed. This aspect alone constitutes a "make or break" consideration when discussing the potential of a successful execution. If for sake of this evaluation, I except the seizure as valid, then I think this technique could be a valuable asset.

49

The physical chain of events set into play by the wrist-grab-hand performing what is basically an arm-drag, the shock and balance displacement of the downward/rearward body-mass forearm strike into the collarbone, and the ankle-trip locking-out the opponent's inability to recover their balance is quite sufficient to support a takedown.

I also like that the rotary motion of the take-down as would most likely land the opponent to the combatant's left. This would support a follow though boot or stomp to downed opponent. If the hold on the assailant's knife-hand-wrist retained [*which it should be] then there are even more follow-ups available.

Chris: I think instead of grabbing the wrist. I would trap it and strike. Most likely chin jab instead of hammer fist, although that would work too. A hammer fist to the nose or chin. Always risky to grab the knife bearing limb… if not grabbed and controlled properly, then the stronger man is gonna win. But if you deflect it or trap it, as you strike, or a split second before, you're probably better off.

Jerry: Never done quite like this, attacker is oncoming high or mid-level, weapon, swing to side step in trap, pull weapon hand to step again if need to palm strike with the back leg take down finish strike very dangerous if they have a weapon the collar blow would probably fix that, one to practice with.

Cris: A modified outer reaping throw (Judo's Osoto gari), with the inside leg behind the other man's leg, you have a variety of options on how much force to apply. You can either go for a simple trip, maintaining your grip on the wrist to control the knife, or kick back to reap out the leg (visualize your leg as a hockey stick) to more forcefully plant him on the ground.

Tommy:

As this is essentially a grip and a reap, it's workable. But not advised.
You want decent control when a weapon is in play. I wouldn't trade a throw to the ground (where he can keep the knife) or a punch to the collarbone (which may not have any effect at all) for decent control with a 2 on 1 grip.

This focuses too much on a strike which is unlikely to take his consciousness. Taking a man's balance is fine, but if he has a knife, you want his life or his light's out and nothing else will do.

Recovering Your Advantage After a Fall

No. 9. Recovering Your Advantage After a Fall

If in a hand to hand encounter you fall to the ground maneuver to land on your side. With the foot that is nearest the ground hook your opponent's heel with your toe. Maintaining this grip stamp sharply with your other foot against the knee of his leg that is so held.

This result is almost like magic. Your assailant will crash prostrate to the ground or the chances are that he will have a broken knee.

Be particularly careful when practicing not to kick out too severely.

> **Bob:** Helps to know something about falling and how to fall correctly. Once you are on the ground and you kick out like that you want to recover as soon as possible with a tactical get up.

52

The leg creates distance. Get your hand up in front of you creating more distance while you use the other hand to assist in lifting yourself up off the ground.

Would be helpful to know some ground fighting if this one doesn't pan out though because if you miss with that kick then the next step is he's going to start kicking you and stomping you out or he will be on top of you and you will be on your back. Better to be on your back then have the back of your head turned toward him or he puts you in a strangle hold and it's night night.

Barry: This a technique that offers circumstantial potential. Potential in that if successful it is capable of maximum results. Circumstantial in that this technique requires an unpredictable fall that lands the victim in a particular post-fall-position relative to a particular frontal position of the opponent.

Circumstance also demands that the angle of flexion of the targeted knee-joint is suitable to allow a forced hyper-extension of the joint. This with the understanding that in order guarantee a break [*which is actually a dislocation] the kicker's foot has to push the knee-joint 6"- 8" through and past the point-of-full-extension. The opponent's foot must also be a weight-bearing foot and fairly well committed at the moment of execution so that it does slip-out with the force of the kick.

If you kick the knee, when the angel of flexion does not support a forced hyper-extension; the knee will not collapse. In this case the only obtainable break is to the knee-cap. This isn't minor, a fractured or displaced knee cap is a serious injury, it just isn't the described outcome.

Given the above-mentioned considerations and assuming that the nature of the scenario disallows getting back-up, I would advocate that the optimal ground-position instead of frontal would be one where the combatant lies at a 45odegree angle out-to-the-side of the opponent.

Employing this angle will support a quicker, shorter-distanced, lock-out of the knee-joint. In turn, this would increase the potential of achieving a debilitating injury.

Jerry: Good technique. I personally had trouble with the timing of the top kick jam knee and the other hook ankle leg.

Faked high slide in low to a variation of this to a scissor throw, also worked against a high mid-level club or knife although more of a sacrifice technique due to danger of going to ground after scissoring the leg takedown. My 2 cents.

Chris: I've seen this done in many different "systems". I'm still of the belief and thinking that you gotta get up as fast as you can and that should be your first priority.

If you gotta keep the guy away from you, some quick piston like kicks to the knee caps would work. I would use this as a last resort if the guy was already too close.

Tommy:

Hate this one. For me this is time wasted that could be spent on getting back up, pulling into a decent guard or up kicking the hell out of their face as you attempt to get up.

The fall the standing guy has is typically on top of you anyway (which isn't great), and most people that move have the wherewithal to avoid.

So this one not on my list.

Cris: If you can get the timing and distance correct, a devastating takedown. You may want to try repetitive kicks with the upper leg to keep opponent's distance, while setting up for this takedown.

Belt Hold And Arm Thrust

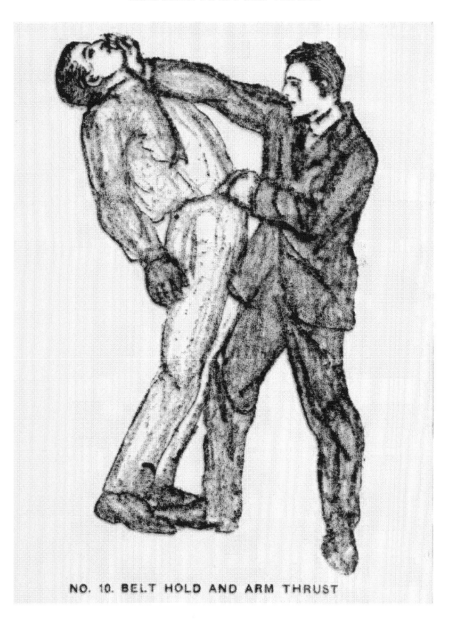

NO. 10. BELT HOLD AND ARM THRUST

In close encounter grasp your antagonist by the belt, or clothing in that vicinity, with one hand and jerk him toward you suddenly. At the same time thrust the heel of your hand with a straight arm movement to his jaw. The blow to the jaw, together with the pull at the belt, gives you the power to crash your enemy to the ground with paralyzing effect.

You will be amazed at the effectiveness of this maneuver the first time you practice it.

Bob: Matt Temkin (WW2 combatives and point shooting instructor) demoed this one once. It can be seen in Do Or Die. Totally effective. Grab the belt and pull and chin jab at the same time. The person is not going anywhere. Their head gets snapped back. Pretty vicious variation of the chin jab where the hand is usually placed around the small of the back.

Also of note here because the instructor from these series of articles was an instructor in the Marines. I have to dig a bit further to access dates but Biddle trained the Marines and also the FBI.

The article is from the 20s so that means that this technique was already being utilized. I have to check when the first printing of Do Or Die was, but I believe that was the 30s.

First Do or Die was printed in 1937

Barry: In reviewing this technique there is a bit mysterious in its workings. It appears to be a basic force counter-force set-up where the pull amplifies the force of the palm thrust. Of course, this equation is in play, but it is not the entire game.

Under scrutiny we note that when yanked, the position of the belt [or clothing in that area] acts upon the body in the exact same manner as when a bouncer gives quick pressure/push to the lower back of an unruly client. In

56

both cases the applied force immediately displaces the balance.

Whereas the bouncer uses this state of off-balance to keep the client moving, the belt hold and arm thrust uses it to set-up the opponent for a topple instigated by the palm thrust displacing the opponent's center mass [located in the upper body] further rearwards. The combined result a potential stun from the thrust and a takedown via displacement of balance.

On a side note; we must include that any momentary shock resulting from the thrust striking/accelerating the brain will disable the opponent thus further robbing them of their ability to resist or counter.

All-in-all it is a handy technique.

Tommy:

Ahhhh the old school obi nage (though there are several throws of that name too). A great technique for muscling people out of a room or a space. Also done well and explosively in sumo.

Does rely on sturdier trousers or belts, but the effect is brilliant when engaged as your balance centre is completely messed up.

Cris: A great setup for a devastating leg sweep, you have broken his balance in a backwards direction, a quick hooking action with your leg (either from the inside or the outside of his leg) will have him crashing down to the ground.

Jerry: Good surprise technique key word you must surprise enemy to work must have balance yourself step in lt foot grabbing with left hand pull striking with right straight arm palm or under chin uppercut strike

It is a must to have a firm grasp of belt or pants Which I personally have had difficulty with at times I like a variation I know as the devils palm where you brace the back of opponents head with lead hand and/or pull head into reverse palm strike to sandwich head I also like the lead hand to brace under opponents arm the shoulder blade s in close to palm strike tiger claw.

Chris: I like this. I teach and train it with chin jab, or tiger claw. And as mentioned above, you could very easily step into a leg takedown.

Jerry: Good surprise technique, key word you must surprise the enemy to work, must have balance yourself step in it foot grabbing with left hand pull striking with right straight arm palm or under chin uppercut strike.

It is a must to have a firm grasp of belt or pants which I personally have difficulty with at times. I like a variation I know as the devils palm where you brace the back of the opponents head with lead hand and or pull head into reverse palm strike to sandwich head I also like the lead hand to brace under opponent's arm the shoulder blades in close to palm strike tiger claw.

No. 11—Rear Strangle Hold

This hold, and most of those which follow, can be used after you have taken the offensive in hand-to-hand conflict. Study the illustration closely, for much depends on the accuracy of this hold.

From a position in the rear of your opponent, throw your right arm over his right shoulder with the large bone in your forearm under his chin, and press tightly against what is commonly called the "Adam's apple."
Rest your left arm pit on top of his left shoulder close to his neck and grasp the muscle of your left arm with your right hand. Then place your left hand at the back of his head.

Apply the strangle hold by forcing his head forward with your left hand and tightening your left and right arms.

Bob: I was taught the variation where you put your forearm against the windpipe and clasp the hands and pull in for a quicker choke. The stranglehold is a classic. Everyone's doing it.

Barry: This strangle hold is an interesting installation. I find that failure is rare as an after-fact of the being installed. As a prefix to its installation, I find failure to be accounted for by the method entry.

It is within this note that I draw attention to the instructions of how to install the initial forearm across the neck. I call attention the choice of words in that they say "throw the arm over his right shoulder with the large bone in the forearm under his chin". To throw by definition is to "propel with force".

Applying this installation as defined would suggest that the intention is to throw the forearm over the shoulder and in under the chin "with force". If this is done then the intention is that they installation itself is party to the injury. Wonderful stuff this, as it robs the opponent of the chance to thwart the hold by wrestling the incoming forearm.

In terms of achieving success, violent blunt-force-trauma to the larynx-trachea joint [just below the Adam's apple] by the incoming "thrown" forearm can be closely

60

the equivalent of an edge-of-the-hand blow. This trauma in itself can be a problem solver where the choke and associated secondary crush are the icing and cherry upon the cake.

These elements alone make this particular instruction stand-out as substantial.

Cris: Today this is more often taught as a blood choke, positioning elbow below the chin to apply pressure on both sides of the neck.

There is a danger of causing permanent damage to the throat/larynx when applying pressure directly on the larynx.

Jerry: This was one of the first stand up jujitsu chokes I learned when I was about 12 years old that worked for me. We called it a get behind. The attacker is on coming with reaching grab strike deflect and or sidestep or shuffle get behind attacker to apply cross arm choke, one may use attacker's body to shield against 2nd attacker.

Chris: THis is a classic in pretty much every system. The problem I think is that it is most often taught wrong or it is not applied to the "Tap" so most people don't know that it actually does work if its taught and trained correctly.

It's risky though which is why it's banned in just about every law enforcement agency in the country. It's effective if done right. MOst of the time it's not.

Michel:

I was taught to smash my forearm in the windpipe and then continue driving until I got to the other side of the neck where I can sink my wrist in the crook of my waiting arm.

You can also start the technique by pulling the individual's hair from the top of his head, jerking him backward, breaking his balance and opening his neck.

If he is follicully-challenged, you can cover his nose and pull back (not below as you may get bit).

Tommy:

This unwisely uses a blood strangle method to cause an air choke. That is difficult to say the least.

When applied to the sides of the neck, as we all know, this makes perfect sense.

Trying to pressure the adam's apple with it is strange and takes a long time to fulfill.

The book would have been well advised to explain the time an 'air choke' takes (quite long) and the importance of balance as the enemy will thrash and buck like a landed shark.

Body Hold

NO. 12. BODY HOLD

This is the proper way to capture a fugitive who has his back turned.

Bob: First of all who's capturing any fugitives? Not me. Who back in those days was capturing fugitives besides some posse or the law? Don't be a hero!

But seriously though, I suppose it's effective until it's not. There are ways to counter this. One simple one is an edge of hand blow to the nuts. I've seen some other interesting ones demonstrated too

Mike: Yeah, maybe safely done with a partner to assist you as he starts to fight back or try to escape. Also this is almost certain to end up on the ground in a real scenario.

Chris: Prelude to a lift and dump!

Barry: What seems simplistic, is in my view a preliminary hold, as alone it offers nothing except an immediate but momentary advantage.

In terms of immediate advantage, the technique offers a reasonably strong momentary constriction/arm-control-capture. This capture must be leveraged into an instant follow-up that provides a considerable increase of control. Viewed in this specific light, there is a scope of armed and unarmed scenarios where its sudden application could be useful.

Follow-ups to consider will be determined by the specifics of the situation, and the intent of the person performing the follow-up.

For a smaller-lesser powerful person, a sweep of the leg(s) may be the cure, or a stomp to the back-of-the-knee. For those with power, a throw down into or onto something is a workable next step. In either case, a vicious bite to the opponent's nearest shoulder/upper-arm would throw a little chaos into their mind while at the same time setting-them-up [distraction] for one of the previous follow-ups.

Following on the aspect of "down, into, or onto something"; if the assailant was armed and the surroundings favorable, a twist/shove down a flight of stairs or out into oncoming traffic may be a solution.

In another scenario, one of multiple threats/opponents, a quick grab and body-hold of one of the opponents could provide a momentary body-shield/obstacle that in its effect could gain a moment of thought, or an avenue of transition.

In a close-quarters space [e.g. public washroom or elevator] this body hold could provide a quick twist/shove that puts an assailant against the wall. This then would offer an opportunity for a very quick grab-n-bash of the opponent's head into the same wall.

So in short; good initial move if you can transition. Crap if that is all you got.

Tommy:

Should be mindful to drop your bodyweight and remind viewers on the danger of interlacing fingers, and ensuring they use a grip like a gable, or wrist grip.

And most importantly, move into the 'then what' of this scenario. How to dump someone or how to position them to a wall or other object and work from there.

Cris: A good way to lift and dump someone, remember, lift with your legs, not your back.

Michel:

To me, it's a prelude to a throw. Setting your foot on the outside of the opponent's foot and twisting in that direction should trip him over, or it may not.

Speed makes all the difference. I don't think it's a good idea to just try and hold on to someone this way.

Rear Trip

LESSON NO. 13—REAR TRIP

This is a very effective way to floor your opponent when you have gained a position behind him.

Slip your left hand under his left arm pit. Lift upward with your left hand so that this weight is thrown on to his right foot with your own and as his whole weight will be resting on that foot, he will be thrown heavily to the ground.

The element of surprise will be your strongest ally in this attack as in many other cases. The chief advantage in all of these holds, in fact, lies in their unexpected application.

Bob: I posted a video once in RATS of FBI agents training probably around the same time period as the articles, where they do this tactic. The main takeaway from this article is "the element of surprise will be your strongest ally in this attack as in many other cases. The chief advantage in all of these holds, in fact, lies in their unexpected application."

So with this technique for example, if he's running away and you catch up to him trip him. But truthfully unless something really fucked up has occurred, why give chase? Again don't be a hero. I think this technique as described is if the creep is just standing there with his back turned, but if that were the case not sure I'd waste my time on this one a stranglehold might be better.

Barry: I don't like this technique. The mechanics of it are too awkward for me and subject to height/mass proportionality.

Certainly, the theory behind this technique is sound, and it would probably work well with equal sized men or when the larger of two men is executing the trip. For smaller and/or weaker statured people I see an avoidable level of failure.

67

Failure for smaller or weaker statured people can come on several forms.

First; due to range and length-of-leg, a smaller person has to get closer to the rear-outside of the targeted leg to ensure a workable ankle-hook.

Secondly; this would then make the reach-out more with their opposite hand to lift the opponent's left armpit/shoulder.

Third; the weaker person may not; a) be able to hoist the opponent in a manner sudden enough to Introduce an element-of-surprise, and/or, b) be able to hoist the opponent in a manner sufficient enough to shift the opponent's weight to their opposite foot.

All of these can be avoided by utilizing another more effective technique.

Tommy:

Like a weird backwards Kosoto-gari. Not for me this one. A bigger stronger man will just keep on walking and throw you by that act.

Only tends to work more like a grapevine, if a bodylock is applied at the same time – but even then it drags you to the floor too.

Hip Break

LESSON NO. 14—HIP BREAK

Notice the position in the illustration above. The head had been snapped back by grasping the chin with one hand, the forehead with the other. At the same instant the right knee has been caved in by a vigorous kick.

69

When the kick is administered to the back of the knee, as illustrated, the hands put a downward pressure on the head crashing the man helpless to his knees.

Practice this attack cautiously and do not resist the hold as serious injury might result.

Bob: You probably need this for when the creep from that basic judo wrist grab technique article kidnaps your girlfriend and you need to rescue her from white slavery. This is when you need to take out that sentry guarding that high priced bordello she has been sold off to.

This technique was demonstrated to me by a friend who was a court officer, as a takedown. One of the few he said he has ever utilized in his career. I've seen it done in conjunction with a stranglehold too which is totally effective. I just can't imagine why it would be needed for a "self-defense" situation though as in this article.

Barry: This is a good technique. It is useable in any situation when facing the opponent's back. As a high-control takedown, it offers a range of uses and a range of severity in terms of its execution and its subsequent outcome. The control over the severity is a direct function of the force put into it.

The inclusion of the simultaneous head maneuver results increased control. This specific execution of yanking back the head [*average weight 14 pounds] offsets the vertical centerline balance which in turn reduces the effort required to kick-out the knee.

Mechanically, the combination of rearward-upper-force and forward-lower-force allows the knee to be vigorously kicked-out. However, it also allows the knee to be pressured into position, or opposite, stomped viciously into the ground.

The hand position on the jaw and forehead also allows for a rapid follow-up application of a head twist should the combatant desire greater injury or to turn the opponent facedown.

The technique offers a strong base in terms of maintaining continuous control. It enables an opponent to be dropped down directly in front of and between the knees of the combatant. From here the assailant can be easily dispatched with any one of a number of methods.

Cris: I'm not a fan of this, too easy to cause more damage than intended. As well, when kicking out a leg, for a split second you are standing on one leg, while balancing not just your own weight, but that of the person whose balance you just upset.

Taking away someone's balance while you have their neck to control their body is a recipe for disaster.

Tommy:

It does the job, but if I'm behind you, I'd rather strangle you than apply this weak crank. In fact calling it a crank is too much praise.

If you've got the back, strangle them unconscious or hold them and pulverize the kidneys. Standing on a knee may drop them down for a second or two, but they'll fight and squirm like hell to get back up because of a lack of body control.

Chris: At the core of it, yes, it could work. I agree though with what Cris said above… If you get a sudden body drop, it's gonna be tough to maintain control of them. There are better ways to put someone on his knee and break his balance.

Elbow Break

LESSON NO. 15—ELBOW BREAK

This is a hold where quickness of action and the element of surprise are paramount. Grasp your opponent's right wrist with your right hand, jerk his arm toward you, twisting the palm side of his arm upward. Then place your left arm under his right elbow grasping his arm with your hand.

Quickly swing your back against the front of his body with your left shoulder under his right, retaining your elbow and wrist hold with your hands.

By "heaving" forward you can snap his elbow and toss him clear over your head so that he will land on his back in front of you, absolutely done for.

Bob: It's a little too involved this one. You can definitely break the elbow if you catch someone's arm like that. Just push the elbow up. Again this presupposes that you are able to achieve the element of surprise somehow against someone wielding a knife after they have already achieved the element of surprise against you…

It's tricky to pull this off and depends on the level of commitment of the attacker. If they want your wallet and that's all they are after, give them the wallet. If it is some psychopath off their meds on the subway, trying to kill you for kicks, you have got to do something.

Mike: Somehow I think the only one using the element of surprise in most situations is the person using the knife.

Tommy:
Can work, but soon as that elbow turns, even a smidge, and it's all over.

Your back in turn and two hands are plunging a knife into your sub-clavian.

I see this as an incidental move mid grapple at best. And most people lack the strength to pull of the dislocation

73

with the force it needs. It's not that easy to break and arm that doesn't want to be broken

Chris: I've seen this in many systems. I've always questioned the viability of it and if it could actually work. Breaking the arm? I'm not so sure. A hyperextension, possibly. I've never trained it so I can't really comment for sure. Just seems a little ineffective and hokey to me. There are better things you could do.

Mike: Agree, locks like these work well in demonstrations. Against a determined knife wielding maniac, either run, improvise your environment, and if you are to engage empty handed get him on the ground and control that weapon or eliminate from the situation. Don't mess around with silly come along holds when there is still a knife in hand.

Barry: I have little time for this technique.

Although I am sure that it will work and work well. I just don't see the value when under the exact same circumstances and initial execution.

I could opt for Applegate's much simpler equally effective flying-mare. While the flying-mare is also quicker, its flow is less complicated. Therein it also offers a reduced under-stress margin-of-error.

Cris: A serious technique as a counter to a deadly technique. For those with a wrestling background, a little extra pressure on the elbow, and a backwards hip thrust will make this into a flying mare, wrestling's famous throw.

Michel:
This would be extremely difficult to apply in a "dynamic engagement."

Jerry: I've never felt comfortable with this one for there are other techniques that don't turn your back to your attacker especially in arms reach, especially with a weapon.

At least the defender has turned to the outside of the attacker's right arm with the defender's left shoulder (if one moves to the inside or the center line of attacker and defender. The attacker's left hand can still attack striking or grabbing.

Also I never felt comfortable with the throw when one can just break the attacker's elbow by straightening up the defender's body and pulling straight the knife arm and slamming it 3 inches above (toward attackers shoulder) the elbow joint over the defender's shoulder. Snap! Follow up as needed.

Head Twist

Lesson No. 16—Head Twist.

When struggling desperately face to face and close to your opponent, suddenly seize his chin with your left hand and the back of his head with your right.

Twist his head sharply and vigorously. The neck muscles cannot withstand a twisting attack of this nature. Your assailant will either be thrown to the ground, or if he resists your hold, his neck will be badly injured.

Bob: This one Chris and I used to train. The other one is the ranger choke. This one seems to have held up as a technique for a long time.

I've seen pictures of people learning this in basic training at boot camp in the 70s. We were doing a seminar once at this dojo in Queens hosted by a guy who used to be in RATS. He said people can get injured pretty badly with this technique because of the twisting action and to use extra caution when demoing it. Has to do with the way the feet were planted or something. I prefer the ranger choke takedown. The throat is a lot easier of a target area to get to. It's usually left exposed.

Chris: Yep, like it, teach it with the takedown.

Barry: I like this technique. Done with the element of surprise and forceful vigor, it is simple and very effective. One asset it offers is that it can executed from any of the 360 degrees of angle surrounding a standing opponent, from many of the available angles when attacking an opponent who is bend over in some manner, and from several angles when dealing with the variations of position associated with a ground-fighting scenario. A second asset is that it can be used at arm's-length to kissing-close.

If it has any drawbacks, it is in the area of "willingness-to-injure".

Attempts to soften this technique should be discouraged as they can quickly lead to failure. Softening by nature of the movement demands a slower application and/or a reduced application of force. Range of rotation is also an issue. Either of these issues will sap the method's key assets.

On the other-hand extremely sharp and/or forceful extreme-range-of-rotation twists of the head can easily result in serious injury to the cervical-spine, nerves, and tissues therein. This risk of substantial injury is

77

amplified if body-weight* is introduced into the equation. [* in terms of force added-in, as-well-as in terms of the opponent's own body-weight if they fall during the crank].

Like lethal techniques, the head twist is a valuable asset, saved for the right time.

Jerry: Neck twist must be quick rage. No warning.

Tommy:
Like this, but feel that one hand on the head only works if you're stronger or equal in size and weight.

Have seen smaller people have success with this after a small tweak.

Namely using the inner forearm against the back of the head as the brace and then twisting the jaw.
Works well at high speed with the element of surprise (but hey what doesn't).

Mike: Used something like this twice in real situations, both worked wonderfully. Both men were bigger than me, my tweak was to grab more of the eyes and ears and tilt their head back.

I got free drinks all night for one of the situations but that is best told over a pint.

Cris: A great way to take someone down quickly. Rotating the head smoothly, pushing out and in a circular motion on the jaw, while pulling in a circular motion on the top of the head.

For safety's sake, guide your opponent's head to the ground. One thing that I would change from the drawing is the position of the feet.

I think you have better leverage twisting the head to the outside of opponent's feet, making it easier to trip him, or circle my lead foot behind me, making it easier to take him down.

Body Hold And Arm Thrust

Lesson No. 17—Body Hold and Arm Thrust.

The principle of this attack is identical with a previous lesson called "Belt Hold and Arm Thrust."

However, instead of grasping the opponent by the belt, throw one arm about his waist and draw him sharply toward you at the same time applying the heel of your other hand violently against his jaw.

This is a very simple method of attack, but is extremely effective.

Bob: I am not a fan of holding onto somebody close like that like they are a dancing partner to execute the technique.

I prefer the combo I was taught of tiger claw, tiger claw, chin jab. Or the one where you throw a chin jab at them and ram it straight through like you are taking their head off with it and sending it to the moon, that's a great one too. I personally prefer the edge of hand blow to the chin jab but everyone has their go to techniques and their own reasons.

Tommy:
I like the attached version like so for use against someone I suspect may be drawing a weapon to body check them and foil the draw. If I don't suspect that, I prefer the unattached version (no hold) so that you can keep smashing them up.

Barry: In reviewing this technique there is a bit mysterious in its workings. It appears to be a basic force counter-force set-up similar to what we saw in the No.10 Belt Hold and Palm Thrust technique. Of course, we also note they both employ a chin jab styled palm thrust.

Here as in No.10, we can support the theory that the palm thrust is thrown in the same manner as a chin jab by scrutinizing the language between No.10 Belt Hold and Arm Thrust and No.17 Body Hold and Arm Thrust, we are told the arm movements are identical, and studying their accompanying illustrations makes a strong suggestion that by accident or intention No.17 illustrates the starting position of the thrust while No. 10 illustrates the finishing position.

Putting word to suggestion it would be sound theory to surmise that arm thrust is executed in a manner closely to, or resembling a Chin jab.

The remaining part regarding the seizure around the small of the back doesn't support a theory of creating an off-balance situation but rather one of stabilizing the opponent to better deliver the palm thrust.

As with No.10, No.17 presents itself as a sound method of attack.

Cris: Arm thrust or chin jab, an excellent up close technique. The opposite hand pulling the opponent in keeps the power of the strike going in one direction, with the opponent not being able to step back, thereby changing the angle of the strike. The restraining hand can also be an open hand strike to the kidneys, adding a little "extra" to the technique.

Chris: I like this. It's a good way to do the takedown with the chin jab push. And it allows a bit more control. Plus, I've seen the arm around the rear of the waist aid in the angle of the bend of the person backwards.

Crotch Hold and Arm Thrust

Lesson No. 18—Crotch Hold and Arm Thrust.

This is a hold that will put you opponent out of the way for a long time. Strike him sharply across the "Adam's apple" with your left forearm, at the same time grasping his left shoulder with your left hand.

Simultaneously, throw your right arm into a crotch hold as illustrated and with a quick movement of your body you will have him upside down. Then crash him head foremost to the ground and you can imagine the results.

It does not take great strength to pick up a man and reverse his position with this hold. A small man can do it readily with a man many pounds heavier.

Cris: A great example of leverage making a lift easier. The secret is of course to bend your knees and lift your legs, not your back. As well, the deeper in you reach, the easier the lift becomes. If you attempt this from a shallow hold (monkey steals the peach), you are essentially doing an arm curl with the other person's weight.

If you can reach deep enough to grab his belt from the rear, he is essentially resting on your bent elbow, and you have eliminated the wrist action and elbow action from the lift.

Straighten your legs, pull the body sideways with your other arm which has grabbed his lapel, shirt, throat or whatever is convenient, and it is easy to spike him on his head

Barry: As a person-of-small-stature, I have no time for this technique.

It fails in three fundamental areas; my interpretation of universally usability, my acceptance of risk of execution vs outcome, and my acceptable failure vs recovery potential.

84

It also fails on my scale of universally applicability as there are just too many external failures just waiting to slip-in. Slippery surfaces, ground obstacles, second man interferences, accidental trips, can all spell disaster.

Like all fulcrum-based-movements poor execution and/or displaced balance can spell injury to the lower-back. This one seems particularly susceptible. I'll leave this one for the experts.

Chris: Nope. Looks like a WWE move. On the street in a fight, you gotta keep it simple and easy... this looks like it is neither.

Tommy:

As a larger chap, I can use this easily.

But when I'm older? Maybe not.

And the end output will be devastating. So it's high level of force and requires high levels of strength. But it feels bloody marvelous when you do it. Important to note how key the knees are to this and ensuring you bend from a squat and not from your back.

Biddle demonstrating belt hold and arm thrust, The Pasadena Post, Sunday August 2nd 1942

Jack Dempsey and unnamed Judo instructor, Popular Mechanics, September 1930

Dempsey tells how Weak or Frail Person May Subdue Bully or Beat Stronger Man

It is possible for a poorly muscled man, or even a frail, delicate woman, to subdue a giant bully.

All that is necessary is the knowledge of a few tricks which will temporarily cripple a thug, even more effectively than a terrific smash on the jaw.

In a series of articles, all illustrated with poses or diagrams, I am going to show just how those tricks can be done. There will be many of them, each designed for different occasions or different conditions which may confront you from time to time during life.

Get Them All.

The simplest pair of tricks imaginable—something that child can do as well as an athlete adult—will be explained in the instalment. A little school girl, properly executing these little stunts, could cripple me temporarily almost as completely as could the most powerful blows of my ring rivals.

In other articles, the tricks outlined will be just a bit more complicated. To learn how to do them really well it is advisable that they should be practiced with someone until the whole action is perfect in execution and lightning-like rapidity.

So why not arrange to team up now with your wife, your daughter, your son, your brother, your father, or some friend, for the purpose of doing the tricks together—that is, the slightly complicated ones, which need a little practice to acquire perfection.

Two vital rules must be kept in mind at all times when attempting each and every trick. They are:

1. Lightning speed in execution.
2. Your body, through the use of your legs, must be perfectly balanced.

    Don't forget either of those vital principles at any time—Speed and Balance. For the success of any trick where a big bruiser or thug is to be overcome, depends on surprising him, if you hesitate, even momentarily, in the complete execution of a trick, you will lose out.

    And if your legs aren't steady and solid, you'll likely lose your balance with the suddenness of your action—and the trick will fail.

Speed and Balance.

So, if you intend to school yourself in the tricks, which I guarantee will make it possible for you to cripple a thug sufficiently to enable you to make a getaway from his immediate neighborhood, please make these definite, sincere resolves at the outset:

"I will practice the stunt of keeping my body in balance at all times."

Work Fast and Use All Your Strength

But Don't Let Him Notice You Sizing Him Up, Is Jack's advice in His Second Article

If a thug or bully confronts you and begins to threaten, there are quite a few things which you can do to render him hors du combat long enough for you to make your escape.

I know of no simpler tricks to accomplish the purpose than these:

1. Kick him lustily on the shin bone; or
2. Stamp your heel upon his toes with crushing force.

If either of those things are accomplished for by you, it'll hardly be necessary for you to run to make your escape. For no man lives who can take a stout kick on a shin bone or a heel smash upon his toes and continue to feel full of fighting, or running—or anything other than terrific pain.

The best part of the kick on the shin, or the stamp of the heel trick is that ta little girl can do it just as neatly and effectively as a giant.

Of course, the smaller and lighter the foot, the less power there'll be in the kick or the heel crush.

But the shin bone and the toes are so sensitive that even a comparatively mild kick or stamp of the heel will create as much damage as is necessary to take the fight out of a bully.

But in the execution of either trick, these things must be kept in mind at all times.

1.   The moment the thug or bully starts his argument steal a quick downward glance at his legs and feet so that you know exactly where they are planted. But don't take too long a look—and don't take more than one all-embracing look. For the thug may sense your purpose and attack you before you try the kick or the heel smash.

2. Be sure your body is perfectly balanced when you kick or stamp the heel. If it isn't you are likely to stumble or fall yourself, from the action.

3. When you decide to kick or stamp with your heel, do it with all the speed and force that's possible.

4. The instant you have kicked the thug's shin bone or crashed your heel onto his toes, step away from him. For it's almost a certainty that he will double up toward you from pain—and if you are within reach, he may grab you.

These tricks need a little practice to make perfect your action. You can practice them with some relative—but when you do, DON'T WEAR SHOES. Do them in stockinged feet, with a few wrappings of cloth around the kicking foot and also around the foot that is to be stamped upon.

By practice you can, in a very short time, school yourself so well that the most fleeting glance will apprise you of the exact location of your enemy's legs and feet. And also by practice you can perfect yourself in a body balance, speed, kicking accuracy and the final trick of stepping away.

Mike: Good targets that are nearly always exposed.

Michel:

A kick from an old school leather wing tip would hurt as it is extremely hard and narrow. Today's running shoes may not have the same effect, even though it would certainly get one's attention.

I would add that hitting with the inside of the foot (as in a cross kick to the opponent's mid-shin and scrapping down to stomp the top of his foot would bring two nice things together. Once again an old school wing tip would definitely make a difference, most certainly ripping skin on the way down.

Bob: I love shin kick techniques. I was told that the way to do it is to visualize scraping shit off the bottom of the shoe. That's how you do the kick. Scrape the shit of the show and make it a kick and land it right on the shin. It sucks. We all know what it feels like to hit a coffee table with our shin by accident.

Cris: Big fan of shin kicks, added bonus, as mentioned if struck with the leather sole of a wing tip shoe (or cowboy boot). Scrapping down the shin and stomping on the foot is a natural follow-up. Surprising how much power you can generate in a very short distance with this kick. Also helps that the shin (and foot) are very sensitive areas to be struck.

Jerry: Side shin kicks. Distract the aggressor and sets up for other finish technique, you can also throw out a shin kick to keep the attacker at a distance but there again one needs to have another technique in the same thought cross kicks are good.

Now with foot stomps shin kicks I think one must consider the kind of shoe one wears. I've heard my grandpa say "give 'em the boot" a heavy hard surface or sole not tennis shoes or sandals or flip flops.

On a different note I learned from my dad when someone is mouthy just step in on their foot or toes when they react by surprise and or pull away then unleash a over hand right to the bottom and pursue as needed.

Tommy:

A shin kick will nearly always take someone's attention down low for a second. Which is a great time to finish with a strike, use a weapon (improvised or not) or make good on an escape when that attention drops for the millisecond. As with all things, it will only take attention away for but a moment. So spend that moment wisely.

Chris: The shin is a very effective target. I love the shin kick – either done as a front kick type of kick or an oblique kick. A great target.

Speed And Wrist Twist A Sure Counter-Attack When Threatened With Weapon

Look at the diagram at the top of this story. A thug armed with a knife is about to attack you. Looks like a dangerous position for you to be in. But it isn't anything of the sort if you are a quick thinker and rapid in action.

Reach out with your left hand—do it with lightning speed—and grab the thug's forearm about two or three inches below the wrist bone. Remember—not more than three inches below the wrist bone. If you grab lower than that you won't be able to get the needed leverage and the value of the trick will be lost.

The instant you have his right arm halted in its murderous downward stroke, reach up quickly with your right hand and grab him with your right hand over his knuckles.

And then you can do one of two things:

1. Twist his fist around in corkscrew fashion. Do it speedily—snappily. He'll drop his knife and he will howl in pain.

2. Bend his hand downward toward his wrist. Do it speedily—with force.

Practice this trick with some friend or relative until you can do it perfectly with either your right or left hand. In practicing it you'll come to know quickly whether you have grabbed the forearm in the right spot. When practicing these tricks with friends or relatives, keep this thing in mind at all times:

Be extremely gentle with the twisting or bending of your friend's hand because by using too much pressure you are likely to snap the bone with the same ease that you would break a pipe stem.

But if a thug with a knife ever attacks you, he means murder. So you needn't be gentle with him. Put on all the pressure that's possible. Break his wrist if the occasion demands, because if you fail, your life may be forfeited.

In a later article I shall outline a leg kicking trick which can be worked in conjunction with the wrist twister. The two tricks, when effectively accomplished, make it possible for even a weakling first to snap a thug's wrist, and then to toss him so heavily to the ground that a tubful of smelling salts wouldn't revive him.

Cris: When you are unarmed against a knife, anything is better than nothing. I don't like the idea of grabbing a moving limb with a wrist grab, as it is easy to have the thumb hyperextended. Would prefer to sidestep and parry, perhaps using a push pull action on the arm to damage the elbow.

Chris: I agree. Parry and get out of the way. Knife defense is so dynamic and dangerous. My focus would be to get out of the way and incapacitate my attacker in some way.

I wouldn't look for a grab. And if it's a high rage, fully committed downward stab with evil intent and violence of action... you're not grabbing anything.

Just get out of the way and hit if you can. If you can't just keep getting out of the way... far away!

Barry: As I consider method as being performed by average people with a minimum of training, I have no-time for techniques that pit life against snap-grabbing some small target already in motion from the hands of an asocial murderer. This is especially true when such techniques require a repeat snap'n'grab movement before the first snap-grab has been reasonably secured against slip or counter. To further complicate things, this method demands a second almost simultaneous snappy-small-target-grab which then doubles the opportunity for failure.

It has been well argued that a one-handed-capture targeting a precise location on a powerful downward drive is a difficult acquisition. I have done this in a real multi-person street-fight. However, a serious difference was that I did it against a 3-foot length of car-jack-post whose mass and momentum alone creates an extralong reversal-of-direction transition-period, quite contrary to a light-weight knife offering considerably less.

I would suggest that a murderous downward drive with a knife begins with a fairly explosive upwards movement, followed by a momentary stall to reverse direction, and then the much-discussed full-strength body-weight assisted downward ballistic drive. OK, so we target the momentary pause.

The math. It takes the average person one-quarter of a second to react to an external-stimuli. Add the time to locate target, calculate trajectory, execute the double grab, and then execute the secondary twist to achieve a functional lock/pressure/twist. My point this that during this time there has apparently been no discernable reflective reaction on by the assailant

Starting with a presumption of an average skilled person, this specific application has all the hallmarks of technique failure.

Tommy:

Humans, being monkey-like creatures often grab when in danger. So whilst a grip may not be my first choice, it may well be just what happens when faced with sudden danger.

The opportunity window for this technique is very small, and even then is full of risk. But if you find yourself holding that wrist for some reason or other, then ripping and tearing that wrist joint violent is certainly an option, but controlling that arm and being violently percussive is still my core advice.

How Grab at Coat and Kick in Shin Can Render Tough Thug Helpless

A very neat little trick designed to render the thug helpless is illustrated in the photographs which accompany this article.

The bully steps forward. He begins to threaten or menace you. You realize that if he gets his hands in motion and either hits or grabs you it means that you are in a bad way.

Beat him to it.

Shoot your hands forward, grab his coat firmly near the top of the lapel, and even as you grab (which action is shown in the top photo) jerk back his coat and slide it quickly off his shoulders and down to a point on the arms, as shown in the lower photograph accompanying this article.

You have rendered his arms useless. While you hold him in that position he cannot harm you—unless he attempts to take a kick at you. But why let him take a kick at you? Take one yourself—as lusty a one as possible. And kick him right on the shin bone, or, if you prefer, stamp your heel upon the toe of one of the other of his feet.

The entire action can be accomplished in about two seconds—with practice. Try it with some relative. Practice grasping the coat in the right place, first of all. Then practice pulling down the coat. Then perform the two actions in one movement—the quick grab and the rapid pull down of the coat.

When you have achieved perfection in executing that stunt practice the follow-up-which is the kick in the shins. Then, as a climax, go through the whole thing-coat grabbing, coat pulling and kicking. In a short time you will be able to do the whole thing with lightning speed.

After that—well, bring on the thug.

Michel:
> A nice variation if you don't think you can peel the jacket down far enough is to just grab the lapels and pull down hard as you step back with one leg. This aggressive motion should break their balance and you can follow up with whatever strike or throw you are comfortable using to end it.

As a Canadian, I have to say, it's the reverse hockey fight move when you pull the shirt over the opponent's head, binding his arms in the process.

Barry: Here we see the lapel grab as a method of securing and/or stabilizing the opponent. This application offers nothing special over many other methods of gaining the same outcome.

The part that stands-out in this technique is the independent value of the shin-kick itself.

The shin-kick is a very impressive and highly underrated technique. In just the sheer variations of its use, its adaptability to range and movement, and scope-of-force-application, it stands-out as unique. You can literally go from introducing an instant of shock to blasting an opponent's leg right out from under them.

In a similar manner it is very efficient as a destabilizer, a pain-based-distraction, or as an entry into a shin-scrape/instep-stomp.

On the value of the shin-kick alone, I give this technique a massive green-light.

Tommy:

It requires such a specific type of jacket (not too loose, not too tight) to almost be unusable.

But for say a doorman of the period, where everyone is in very similar clothing – I can see why it existed.

Michel:

Having played with it, the key to executing this is to move extremely fast. Also, make sure the jacket isn't buttoned or zipped up.

It will not only depend on the recipient, but on the type of jacket. Best to start it off with that shin kick. I agree with Barry that it's the best part of this technique.

Jerry: I like this like all techniques you adapt. Improvise the technique to the environment or situation from clothing to ice on ground etc. If you cannot trap arms with jacket then check arms especially the weapon arm then knee or head butt and so on..

Chris: I've never really seen this done outside of movies and TV. There is a certain viability to it, but I think the jacket pull would have to be quick and effective the first time.

You're not getting a second chance to pull the jacket without getting whacked.

Goat Trick Effective In Bruising Up Attacking Thug

Here's a little trick that can be worked by grabbing the coat, which not merely will help to foil a thug, but it also will smash up his features.

Grab him by the coat lapel, as shown in the top photograph. Then duck your own head and jerk his face toward you, with all the force that's possible.

Look at photograph at bottom of this article for result.

To make the occasion just a bit more unenjoyable for the thug, aim a kick at his shins just as soon as you have smashed his face against the top of your head. Unless his face and his shin-bones are made of iron, the thug will be so busy nursing his hurts for the next five or ten minutes that he will forget that he is on earth.

This trick needs a little practice to be accomplished effectively and surely. Practice it. But when you do, be sure to pack a lot of cloth on top of your own head when you are pulling the face of your friend into it. Otherwise, your friend will look just like a bully looks when this stunt has been worked on him.

Cris: A true classic. Not questioning its effectiveness, but not a fan of slamming my head into things.

Bob: I read an old article that described this as the Danish Kiss. The Irish kiss as it was described to me is a kick to the side of the thigh.

I learned from someone who trained in his system that the Irish Kiss was a technique that Charlie Nelson taught.

Cris: Hmm and a knee to the side of the thigh (Charlie Horse) is sometimes called an Irish Toothache. Oddly enough, I learned the term from one of Charlie's students.

Bob: Danish Kiss??? Guess it might have been a popular Danish technique. I thought I read, with sailors or something. I have an article where it mentions all these "tricks" and their nicknames. It's an old article discussing dirty fighting tactics boxers use.

As a matter of fact Steiner's article on Charlie Nelson mentions he had a Danish background. He grew up in Bay Ridge which was totally Scandinavian and Irish at one time. It all comes full circle. Not too many Mongolians there though as far as I'm aware.

Michel:

Headbutts are deadly. In case of no jacket, you can work the head butt from the clinch. I also learned to turn the opponent's head to the side after connecting with a lighter version of a chin jab, and then headbutt to the side of the face or temple (no teeth). Lethwei headbutts are made for grabbing the opponent.

Barry: Usable by most everyone, the head butt is a classic. Its use can generate a sharp reflex, to a complete and unexpected knock-out.

Used strategically it can be delivered to the nose to instigate a watering-of-the-eyes, to open the thin skin of the outer eye-brow to instigate bleeding down into the eye, to cause distraction by strike generally into the opponent's face while moving from one action to another. A headbutt delivered just in front of and slightly below the ear an achieve a broken jaw.

When I teach the head butt, it is primarily as a diversion.

When fighting tangled up or fighting face-to-face with an opponent, or when transferring the head from one side of the opponent's head to the other while manhandling or grappling, a quick sharp crack with the head will cause a momentary blip in the opponent's attention. This is of excellent value.

A side benefit of the head butt is that it comes from a chin-down forehead-forward defensive head posture and is executed maintaining the same posture. This utilization doesn't cost expose and can protect the face by making it less accessible. A small benefit that does well when fighting close range.

To increase the sense of violence, or as a method to aid targeting I teach using one or both hands pull the opponent's face into the butt. This secures secured misalignment and allows a bit of a final-grind if and when that option offers benefit.

An excelling complement to the head butt is a menu of random eye attacks, ear slaps, and my all-time favorite, biting.

Tommy:

Love a headbutt.

Always best taught to me to treat as a sneeze. We all know how to sneeze. And when we sneeze we typically engage our neck, shoulder and back muscles.

Students often headbutt lamely. Say sneeze in someone's face and they already know what to do.

Also works very well as a pre throw technique or transitional half beat technique as you keep the pain coming and keep them disoriented.

Jerry: Head butts are fight stoppers best to hold clench or brace and if needed bite nose or ear. They will think twice bout getting close to you.

Chris: There are a lot of people that swear by the headbutt. I have it in my curriculum but it's not a primary technique. A well placed headbutt will definitely stop your attacker you just have to be aware that it may daze you for a second or two as well. Aim the top of your head for the lower part of his face- nose and below.

Prostrate You May Render A Foe Helpless, By Simple Hold On His Trouser Legs

Please take a look at the photograph which accompanies this article.

Johnny Lee is on the floor, having an innocent sort of hold upon the bottom of my trousers. Doesn't look as if he is doing much with that but wasting effort, does it?

Yet Lee has me helpless to make a further attack upon him.

In this particular article, written for the purpose of showing you what you can do if a thug should happen to knock you down. I play the part of the thug, and Johnny Lee, a sparring partner of mine, was the victim.

I dropped Johnny. The minute he hit the floor he grabbed my trouser ends with the fingers of his hands—got a good hold on them by crumpling some of the cloth into the palm of his hands. Then he crossed over with the thumbs of each hand so that four fingers of one hand held one trouser end and the thumb of the same hand was hooked onto the other trouser end.

I was helpless to move. If I tried it Johnny would have jerked my trouser ends and upset me. If I attempted to make a kick he would have pulled forward with both hands at the same time and I would have been lifted off my feet and fallen backward on the back of my head.

This is a trick which needs but little practice, can be easily learned and will be invaluable to you if it happens that a thug throws you to the ground unexpectedly.

But you must practice to get it perfect.

Sometimes it will happen that the thug's legs are spread far apart, which will make it impossible for you to lock his legs as Lee has done in my case. Just grab a trouser and with each hand, stick your fingers as far up the trouser legs as possible. Pull down on the trousers then so that they will be taut.

When you get such a hold you will find how easy it is to jerk the thug off his feet and drop him backwards on his head. All you need to do is to pull him forward with a jerk—both hands jerking at the same time—or suddenly jerk your arms upward.

But, at all times, you must remember to keep a taut hold on those trousers' bottoms. Don't leave any slack. If you do you null the value of the trick.

Barry: Is this really one to review???

Cris: "Kiss my Converse!"

Mike: "Stick your fingers as far up the trouser legs as possible" You might get arrested for that haha!

Cris: It's like he doesn't know his knees bend. If someone is hanging onto your pant legs as shown, drop your knees on their head, or shoulders. Not recommended.

Jerry: Shoe string kung fu.

Chris: Why is this guy on the floor in the first place?

Tommy:
I took the piss too. But actually, it works quite well if you give it a go (assuming you're taking a kicking on the floor). But there's danger for them dropping their knees down on your back. But as a quick disrupter – it "can" do the job.

Quick Grasp, Press Of Left Hand Breaks Arm Of Ruffian

See the little fellow in the picture? Doesn't' look very dangerous, does he?

Yet if he pushed back his left hand merely an inch or so he might end my fighting career.

That's all because of the wonderful trick hold he has secured upon me. It's one which you can get on a thug—if you think rapidly and act quickly.

The way this chap worked it on me is the way which you can work it yourself.

He faced me for a while, and just to make things realistic we got into an argument. I played the part of the thug threatened the little fellow. He faked that he was getting afraid of me and began backing away.

Naturally I figured I had frightened him and didn't anticipate that he'd pull any trick.

But all the time he was backing away he was going slightly sideways— toward my left side. Then, like a flash, he whirled at me, wheeled around so that we both were facing the same way. And also like lightning, he jammed his **right arm** under my left and reached for my right coat lapel, as the illustration shows.

Then he grabbed my left hand with his left—and he had me at his mercy; for, if I had tried to break loose, all he needed to do was to press down, jerkily, with his left hand in the direction of my hip.

The result would have been a broken arm for me.

Try this trick with some friend. It can be learned easily and you'll only need to try it once on your friend—or have him try it on you—to be convinced of its wonderful value in battling a thug or bully.

Barry: I definitely give this one the green-light. However, I do so with a note of caution to it being overly complicated. I would also point to an unnecessary risk that it accepts.

First off, the green-light. This technique offers a functional advantage in enabling a person of smaller stature to forcibly manhandle an opponent of any size. This advantage us gained via a direct application of pressure applied to the opponent's elbow-joint. Simultaneously, it offers an opportunity to quickly dislocate an opponent's elbow-joint. This being a kinder game-ender than breaking his neck or concussively bouncing their brain around the inside of their skull.

Now, to being overly complicated. It has been my experience that opponents rarely remain stationary when their opponent is leaping about to face them on a 45 or off 90 degrees to their side [never mind ending up facing the same direction as them]. This is a lot easier said than done.

Under this acknowledgement, the effectivity of the entry into this move is questionable. Add in the seizing their arm and swinging it up into position; and the opponent is given even more time to react or respond.

The same concern goes to grabbing the opponent's lapel. While this does add latch-point stability to the method, an opportunistic employment element-of-surprise and the opponent's inertia do equally well. As with gaining position, the lapel maneuver provides reaction time and a chance where a missed-grab requires recovery or causes failure.

To the point of unnecessary risk, the most obvious risk is the unbridled addition of time. "Never give a sucker an even break".

The second point may be controversial; but for me, I have far-to-often seen clothing-grabs become finger-entanglements which along with being a critical disadvantage can mean broken or sprained fingers and the resulting deficit in hand-usage.

Under my instruction, I definitely teach this arm-lock/break. However, I teach it in a completely different manner, under completely different circumstances.

First off, as combatants, strategically we are more vultures recognizing opportunity than lions hunting with technique. Under this approach, we do not seek the application of technique but would [for whatever reason] rather find ourselves by circumstance, available to it. By circumstance, a combatant is presented with an opportunity to very quickly apply dislocating-pressure and the immediacy of joint-hyperextension. There is no attempt to lock and hold the arm.

Here, the immediacy of the joint-lock going directly to dislocation, leaves the opponent with zero time to counter. Like the flying-mare, the opponent's only reaction/response options are to saving themselves from the joint-break by going with the maneuver, or accepting the break.

It is under this more aggressive application that I really light-up the green-light.

Mike: I feel like the most important lesson here is not only the technique of the hold, but the set up.

Have a plan, lie, trick, deceive, especially if you are smaller or look weaker. Also worth pointing out the mention of speed in a situation like this, being smaller means you better make Plan A work, if not just hope your in-fighting game is strong.

Michel:
This could be an escape from an aggressive handshake, if you can extend your opponent's arm straight before pivoting alongside him (hip to hip).

114

Cris: Does the technique work? Yes. Is it appropriate for self - defense? I don't think so. Might be appropriate for a bouncer or removing your drunk uncle from a party.

Tommy:

Works much better when moving an opponent than as a "break" per-se. Also for lesser threat door work as an escort which takes away a powerful hand from a potential attacker.

Jerry: This is a technique where you tell the aggressor "hey I'm sorry, please don't, I don't want to fight... come on let's be friends..." All the time extending the right hand for a hand shake as you friendly touch fingers, smiling, grab hand or wrist (your right hand to his right hand) now suddenly stepping with left leg forward into a side stance to attacker simultaneously pulling right hand arm straight now snake your left under the attackers upper arm 3" above the attacker's elbow.

Now with your left hand grab attacker's left lapel to a come along lock or break elbow violently pulling attacker's left arm down over your left secured arm grasping the lapel if they have no jacket lapel or no shirt on to grab them with then turn your left arm counter clockwise palm up – if non-violent stick your thumb into the soft tissue and with fingers and hand squeeze the jaw bone (very painful) or grab the throat squeeze while pulling down with right shaking hand attackers right arm. At any time one violently shake and break this sometimes applies to grappling on the ground.

Chris: I think Fairbairn had this in one of his books. I've never personally trained it, but it does look like it could be pretty effective especially if you are able to trap the elbow joint well. Maybe I'll start training this one...

Break His Strangle Hold With One Hand

Let's suppose someone tries to choke you. He'll reach forward and with both hands, grab at your throat. If he reached the vital spots with strong fingers, he probably could choke you within a very few seconds.

But there's no reason why you should be choked.

Look at the picture. Johnny Lee, my sparring partner. Is the thug for this occasion. Johnny reached forward and clutched my throat with his fingers. But in less than one second he had let loose.

And that's all because I simply grabbed one of his little fingers and pulled it back toward me—with force.

Johnny let loose of that hold on my throat—and so will anyone else when you jerk back the little fingers.

Try the trick yourself—and you'll find the reason why.

Whenever a thug sets upon you and tries to choke you, there are two big things to remember. Pull back the little finger—and then kick him in the shins or stamp your heel upon his toes.

You'll be quite safe then.

Barry: I am at crossroads with this technique.

One side it is clear to me that if you get a solid grip on a person's little-finger that you would be in a position to snap one of its base-joints with relative ease. There is also the anatomical fact that unlike the other fingers, the little-finger has its own nerve. This and that fact that smaller fingers are more sensitive to pain cause it to have greater effect.

I think part of my problem with this release-technique-to-a-double-handed-choke; [an many others like it] is that all too often they deal with the choke being applied in a fairly static stable manner. In contrast, my experience with the application of a double-choke is one of a violent grasp of the victim's neck, arms in full triangulation to maximize force and control, tip-of-the-thumbs dug well in, accompanied by a violent shaking of the victim's head and body in an effort to deter an effective response, destabilize their balance, and generally cause more mayhem and injury. These all go to a greater difficulty in seizing the assailant's little-fingers.

In reflection, I have always had a hard time achieving a quick-solid grip on an opponent's little-finger. Add-in the potential for slippage or a quick counter [many of which do not require releasing the choke] and I would be looking to an alternate cure.

Michel:

Agree. The only thing I can add is that some people are quite flexible and you can bend a digit quite a bit back before it breaks. Fingers break much more easily (and much faster) if you bend them to the side than they do when you bend them backwards.

That being said, it may not be easy to pull off either way if the opponent is stronger than you, his fingers are tight together and digging into your flesh...

Chris: There are definitely better and quicker ways to stop someone choking you.

It takes too much time to reach for and bend back a finger. Not to mention, if they are really, truly choking you, you're not gonna be able to grab and bend finger quickly enough... try it with a training partner.

Don't choke all the way obviously, but get a good enough squeeze and you'll see isolating and bending a finger is actually pretty tough.

I think I mentioned this before, just hit the guy.

Tommy:

Finger breaks have their place. But an attack on the throat is an attack on your life. If the opponent is tough,

118

determined or drugged – he won't feel jack. Spend your time taking eyes, throats and consciousness instead.

Rooted To Spot As You Stand On His Toes

Any time you have the desire to land a punch or two upon a thug—without risk to yourself—it can be accomplished very easily.

All you need to do is to stand upon his toes, as I am standing on those of Johnny Lee. Having done so, chuck your right palm under his chin and push his head backward. He's helpless because your action in standing upon his toes has knocked him completely off balance.

Then if you are eager to take a nice shot at him, all you need to do is to double your right fist and let loose with it. Crack him on the rim of the chin, drop one on his nose or drive one under the heart—anywhere you wish. At the moment you hit, step off his toes quickly and the result will be that you'll score a complete knockdown.

It's well to practice this trick of standing on the other fellows toes for the simple reason that until you have acquired the knack you are likely to lose your own balance by attempting to stand upon them.

> **Barry:** I have no time for this technique. It is far too complicated for a real-life defense against a real-life thug.
>
> As far as standing on toes [one or both]. I was taught a single-foot version in boxing. There, it was taught as a spur-of-the-moment opportunity to stumble the opponent, not a planned intention. Further, I never heard of anyone ever actually doing it.
>
> As far as standing on both toes at the same time. I actually know of only one person who has done it in real-life. If it offers any faith to the faithful, it was done by a Chilean policeman who did it to a guy who was sticking a gun in his face. Here again, it was pure reaction done in a moment of zero-thought and desperation as opposed to anything clever or planned out.
>
> In combat, standing square is a blatant no-no and sure-fire way to disable power generation, and jeopardize balance.
>
> For me this technique is useless if not actually a danger to oneself.

Michel:

I like the palm strike, but I agree that standing on both feet with yours is unrealistic. Even if you could pull it off, you'd lose your balance right away.

In FMA foot traps are common and they work, but only one foot at a time. I like to use it when I spar in boxing just for practice. I can now pin an opponent's foot quite easily most of the time without even looking as you get used to reading the upper body to get an idea where their feet are at all times. Takes practice but once you've mastered it, you can apply it quite consistently.

Cris: Agree, palm strike is good, standing on both feet is unrealistic. Stomp on foot? Sure. Trap foot after stomping? Yep. Then again, if you're this close, why not trap foot and give a hard shove to the chest, knocking him over and breaking ankle.

Bob: Another chin jabby one. He places his shoe on top of and stands "on the other fellow's toes" it is an interesting one but I wonder how likely one would be able to pull that off. Somewhat similar in theory to grabbing the guy's belt, but instead of pulling just keeping him there while you slam his head backwards. I can hear the teeth crunching. Could be a real nasty one if done like that as illustrated.

Mike: I have found myself sometimes accidentally stepping on the foot with this and other moves which have ended up assisting. Not a technique I would aim for as I wouldn't focus on an area likely to miss, but if it happens go with it and make it work.

Tommy:

Power requires balance. It requires some stability.

Standing on people's toes is not stable. Never in a million years would this be the go-to.

Jerry: I like the concept, toe stepping distraction palm strike but not in the method being shown. I also like the idea of setting my right foot inside the attacker's right foot so the palm strike causes him to stumble back over my foot.

Chris: I've seen foot traps and trained them. Agree with Michael above – they are common in FMA – that's where I learned them, but I've seen them in other systems too. A simple foot trap to keep the person from moving away from a technique is an effective technique. I wouldn't step on both.

Quick Action And Little Strength Will Flatten Attacker Effectively

This article details how the average man, even if something of a weakling, can drop a big thug to the ground.

All that is necessary is rapid action. If a thug confronts you, grab him **quickly**—as is shown in the first picture of this article. Then with all the speed you have, whirl him around slightly, or, instead of whirling him, do the whirling yourself. Either way is O.K. if it accomplishes the main idea which is to achieve such a position that your left leg is back of his right leg.

Having done so, kick at the back of his heel. Don't try to kick with your toe. Do it with the side of your foot—with the whole instep, as shown by the second picture in this article.

One solid kick delivered in the right place will drive the thug's leg forward, knock him off balance—and down he goes.

This is another trick which requires a bit of practice. But when practiced even for a little while it can be made to operate perfectly—to the discomfiture of any thug.

Cris: I got to admit, this looks like an interesting combination foot sweep/arm takedown. The foot sweep is a standard judo style foot sweep (Deashi barai), but the arm takedown concerns me as it looks too easy to over twist the elbow/shoulder, making it perhaps a more debilitating takedown then intended.

Barry I like this technique. It is a solid technique. But the fact that it requires an extremely well-practiced quick execution cannot be overstated.

Like the Kimura and the Figure-four, this entire movement hinges on the angular immobility's of the shoulder's ball & Socket joint. The key to this technique is the upper-arms' inability to rise-upwards when the forearm at a right-angle, points downwards. This same posture also greatly limits rearward rotation.

Like the wrist-lock, the technique offers substantial risk of failure up until the point where the shoulder-lock is achieved. Also like the wrist-lock, once the lock is achieved the outcome is almost guaranteed. Speed is of the essence!

Once secured, the most minor rearward leveraging of the forearm will result in immediate pain and if continued severe damage to the ligaments of the joint.

It is important to understand that this technique can be easily defeated by simply stepping-away while extending the arm. Therefore, gaining this arm configuration offer the greatest risk of jeopardy. It is where a practiced quickness is crucial. Equally so, this is where a good plan B should be in reserve.

Once the arm/shoulder lock has been achieved the same quick leverage that locked the shoulder will also quickly break the opponent's balance to where a basic sweep of the foot will bring them down. Perform it with explosive violence and it has full potential will dislocate the shoulder and be a game-ender.

Bob: Sweeping the leg. Solid technique that can work. Kicking the shins and lower limbs, those are good ones too.

Tommy:

Love the technique. Just be sure to get the opponent moving first.

Much easier to pull off if they're stepping about and trying to retain balance. The fall is also not too damaging so be ready to run or finish the job another way.

Mike: I feel more inclined to use my other leg, but he if it works it work.

Chris: This looks a little too complicated and seems like it would have to be "perfect" in order to pull off.

I would stick with the standard leg sweep or trip.

Hammerlock Of Wrestlers Effective Hold At All Times

This twelfth trick is quite simple. Just grab the thug's right wrist with your own right wrist. Then swing his arm toward his back and jerk it upward.

That's about all that's necessary. Of course if you want to be awfully rough with him, grab his left shoulder with your left hand. Push his right arm up a little higher as you do so.

And then—well, just throw him to the ground as hard as you wish.

Or, if he's a real desperate sort of thug, you need merely to exert extreme upward pressure on his right arm to fracture it.

Barry: This is one of those techniques that to me do not belong in a fight. As far as I am concerned it is a come-along technique best suited to control-and-restraint situations.

As far as its value in actual violence, I hold zero respect for submissions and holds because they can't be held indefinitely but end leaving the assailant with full-capacity to re-engage, only now all-the-wiser.

The value they do have is as a transition-technique. One where the controlling-factor of the technique enable a swift transfer to a more damaging application such as an immediate dislocation of the shoulder, a force-to-the-ground-takedown, a rear-choke, a strike, stomp, or other injury.

In this latter case, I give it the green-light.

Jerry: I view this technique as a get behind come along or control technique to direct or redirect the bully or assailant one may slam into vehicle or bump head into wall or by lifting attacker's arm upward high tto take attacker to the ground.

Chris: Great technique for control and movement. Being a trainer of law enforcement, I really like this technique. If applied correctly, it really works and is effective. This is actually one of my favorite control techniques.

You can actually apply it from the front as well and I've seen an old beat cop trick where it's done from a handshake.

There are some variations that can make it more effective and painful that I've seen and trained and taught. Again, one of my favorites.

Michel:

I agree with Barry but I also agree that it can serve a purpose if you move from the lock to a brutal shove against a wall or some type of obstacle. It sends a message that you know how to handle yourself.

I don't think it would be easily applied in a fight. It's more of something you could do when things are beginning to heat up.

Cris: As mentioned by both Barry and Michel, a come-along hold does not belong in a fight. It has its place, but not really self-defense.

Tommy:

Much more securely done as a Figure 4 Hammerlock (or as you crazy kids call it now – a Kimura). Same thing, but much stronger, tighter and safer.

Once you have it on, even if they fall to the ground, you can finish the job too.

Walk Briskly, Breathe Deeply Is Jack Dempsey's Prescription For Health

Among those who have been trying out the trick of repelling a thug's attack was a middle aged man, who wrote:

> "They're great—but I find that I can't do them very well because I'm short of breath after the least exertion. That, of course, knocks me out in a certain way.

> "I'm wondering if you will not, before you proceed with the articles, outline some way in which a man whose muscles are somewhat soft, and who is short of breath, can correct those faults in speedy fashion. I'm sure there are many other of your readers in my plight and all would welcome such a suggestion from you."

So, for today, there'll be no article on thug repelling. Rather, there'll be this one, which will suggest a form of exercise that will help to build up the body so that the performance of the tricks already outlined, and those to come, can be done much easier.

In my years as an athlete. I've experimented with a thousand different methods of achieving physical fitness. But of them all, there's one more effective, none more simple, than this combination:

Brisk walking—Deep breathing.

Everybody walks every day—and everyone breathes many times every minute of the day. Yet there isn't one human out of 100 who gets the real benefit and the good out of walking—and there's not one in 10,000 who derives one-tenth the good that can come from deep and correct breathing.

The trouble with most of us when we walk is that we just amble along. And when we breath—well, we just breathe to keep alive and not with the added purpose of breathing deeply to keep well.

For those whose muscles are soft, whose wind is poor, who always have headaches and always feel sort of groggy, here's the prescription:

Walk at least three miles every day—out in the open air. Walk briskly. Speed it up. Take good long strides. Let the arms swing free and fast as you walk. Keep the head up and the shoulders well back.

The first day you start in for such walking exercise, promise yourself that you will take ten long, deep breathes. Take fifteen the second day, twenty the third, and add five breathes each day until you have reached 100.

After that you can stay at such a figure, or increase it at your will.

How to Breathe Properly.

When performing this breathing exercise, do it in this way:

Fill the lungs slowly—and to their fullest capacity, always drawing in the breath through the nose. Then hold the breath in the lungs as long as you can—and then a little longer than that. When you can't retain the air any longer, exhale—**with force**. Let the air come out through the mouth with the lips forced in a pucker as though you were whistling.

Ten such breaths the first day—fifteen the second—twenty the third— and so on. That's the prescription.

Sounds simple doesn't it—and it doesn't sound as if it will prove wonderfully beneficial when coupled with a three mile brisk walk.

But—try it—just for two weeks. And then—well, you have found one of the most wonderful health recipes in the whole world.

The thug in this particular instance is about to grab the intended victim from behind, but he never accomplished his purpose.

For the "victim" saw the right arm of the thug as it was about to encircle him. Quick as a flash, he grabbed the thug's arm in the way illustrated in the picture.

Having done so, he placed his right foot against the thug's right foot—but he (the intended victim) made sure that **his own leg had the outside position**.

From that moment on the thug was helpless.

Study the picture carefully—and then try the trick yourself. It won't take you long to discover how it's possible to get a thug or bully in your power—if, at all times, when you have secured such an arm hold, you place your leg against the thug's—and have yours on the outside.

> **Cris:** A less refined version of Judo's Tai-Otoshi. Would want to emphasize the pulling of the arm, drawing him into you, then around you.

> **Chris:** If you see the grab coming, sure this would work. The problem is you're not gonna see it coming unless your attacker is completely incompetent , in which case, just about anything would work.

Tommy:
> Essentially a tai-otoshi. Works really well, if you ensure you drop your bodyweight and pull viciously.

> He won't fall over, you have to explode and propel him to the ground. Done with great effect by Judoka's the world over.

Dempsey Shows How to Turn Tables on Attacker From Rear

The picture shows the "victim" using grasp of a thug—to turn the tables on his attacker—He knows the trick of getaway from such a hold.

It's simple, when one grabs you about the neck from the rear. Just bend one knee and push that leg well back between those of the thug.

When doing so be sure to maintain a good balance on your other leg. Your action in shoving back one leg lowers your body. The thug's body follows the movement of yours. That being the case, lower your body quickly—jerkily—and the result is that you'll throw the thug over your head onto the ground.

Bob: Seems like something that could work in theory. Would have to move very fast because if you hesitate he could pull you in the opposite direction and down toward the ground. Or punch you in the lower back with a vertical punch like in Get Tough.

Chris: Seems like you would be off balance a little bit if you actually tried this. As previous techniques, there are more effective ways to deal with an attacker who grabs you from behind.

One thing that is necessary is speed. I'm all about hitting. Hit the guy till he lets go and falls down.

Tommy:

It's a balance breaker for just a second and can leave you off balance and extended.

So be sure to follow up with something else like the body drop throw shown above this technique.

136

The Wrist Breaker Is Simple But Effective In Results

Trick No. 16 is what you might call the wrist breaker. Study it closely.

All that's necessary for you to do to accomplish the trick is to grasp the wrist of the thug as I have grabbed that of Johnny Lee, my sparring partner.

Take a firm hold on the wrist with one of your hands and then bend down his hand as shown in the illustration.

Even pressure will cause tremendous pain. A sudden snap is very likely to break the wrist. So when practicing this with any of your friends, be very careful not to do any jerking.

Cris: A classic restraint, the gooseneck or bent wrist come-along. Fairly easy to setup by inserting your inside arm between his ribs and arm, grabbing the back of his hand with both your hands, like you're holding a sandwich and tucking his elbow under your armpit like you're running with a football. If you don't tuck the elbow, there is a good chance of the elbow flaring out and catching you on the chin, as he attempts to move away from the pain of hyperextending his wrist. For variations, the fingers can be pointed up or down, the elbow can be tucked under the arm as discussed, or pointed straight down for a fast takedown.

Barry: Very little has to be said about this method. It is solid as a rock. The learning curve is miniscule. The retention is forever. And the ability to perform the method goes on well into the grey-hair years.

The outstanding points of this attack are that it is entirely based on opportunity recognition, uses a fundamental grip, can be applied in any number of scenarios, in any number of manners.

By opportunity recognition, I mean all it requires is for a combatant to recognize they are gripping the wrist palm over hand, or to recognize that they in on proximity and position to grasp the opponent's wrist with a palm over hand grip. Nothing else matters other than can grip the wrist or not.

By fundamental grip, I mean this grip is one that is 100% an untrained day-you-were-born grip. Having said this, you can even enhance the grip by the simple act of rolling in the fingers [starting with the baby-finger first] as you wrap your fingers around the hand.

By any manner, I mean applying the strength and angle required to hyper-flex or hyper-extend the wrist-joint to the point where a disabling injury [severe sprain, dislocation, or break] can be forcing the wrist downwards [the easiest], upwards, side-to-side, or any other angel of opportunity. Every one of them is capable of rapidly achieving a disabling injury that will seriously decrease an opponent's ability to fight.

Jerry: Good come along technique. I have never used it but as a police chaplain I have seen it used effectively three different times by officers against suspects. I caution about these locks and come-alongs, continued practice of these with a compliant partner will give one a false sense of security. I believe that if some out of head person doesn't want to be held there is not a lock or hold in the world that can hold them.

Chris: A pretty standard come-along technique. Cris gives a good description above- not much more to say.

"Muscle And Elbow" Hold Puts Attacker At Odds

If you grab the arm of the thug with your left hand as shown in the above illustration, and place your right hand under his elbow in firm fashion, you will have the thug at your mercy.

For all that's necessary to produce pain is to shove up the elbow of the thug while you maintain a firm hold on his biceps.

If you act fast in this manner, it is not a difficult thing for you to do to twist the thug's arm in such a way that his fist will be far behind his back.

When doing this trick, added leverage can be secured by placing your left leg up against his right leg—having your leg occupy the inside position.

Tommy:

The hands are two close to deliver any 'fulcrum' that would trigger the lock.

Simply do not see any anatomic value to this attack. Elbow and wrist, yes, not this.

Bob: I suppose if you caught someone like that fast enough as they are holding their arm and fist up that way and say "I'm going beat you within an inch of your life!" and you quickly jostled them it would throw them off balance and off their game. Not sure why one would want to mess around like that though.

Seems like you are right there hit him with a hand yoke if he's some kind of threat and run. Stun and run!

Cris: Not sure about this technique, strange way to apply leverage, and I don't like the idea of leaving someone's fist in my face.

Chris: I am always skeptical of just grabbing someone without at least stunning them first.

If you grab someone and the grab isn't "just right" the stronger, quicker thinker is gonna win... If that's not you, you're gonna pay the price.

A Strangle Hold the Thug Won't Break

In an earlier article I explained the trick which you could use in case a thug grabs you around the neck. The idea was for you to stick your right leg far back between his two legs and bend over suddenly, thus throwing him over your back.

Now this trick, No. 18, is one in which I demonstrate how you can grasp the thug around the neck, and even though he knows the trick about breaking the hold, you can keep him at your mercy.

In this particular article Johnny Lee is playing the role of the thug. I am the supposed victim. But I succeeded in getting back of him quickly and I caught him around the neck in what might be termed a strangle-hold fashion.

Realizing that Johnny knew the leg trick, which would enable him to throw me over his back, I beat him to it by placing my foot in such a position that I had Johnny blocked off in his efforts to stick his leg between and back of mine.

If you practiced the other trick, it is a very good thing for you to practice this additional one, inasmuch as it gives you double-barreled information as to what to do when someone has grabbed you around the neck or you have grabbed someone else.

> **Bob:** Reminds me of an article about Stirling Siliphant the movie director and a student of Bruce Lee's and he asked Bruce what can you do if someone puts a wire noose around a victim's neck and strangled him. Bruce tells him "You die. The only way out is to not get yourself in that position in the first place. If a good cat gets a noose around your neck, you'll be dead in a matter of seconds because he'll pull you back off balance and you won't be able to get to him."

> **Jerry:** I like this one but you need to understand and be ready cause after the shock and in the painful adrenaline dump they will be really really really Mad with sudden supernatural strength. Be ready to finish it or run.

Chris: I think this was discussed in an above section. A strangle type of hold- any variation- is effective if done properly

Just a Little Speed and Strength Needed to Put an Attacker Hors du Combat

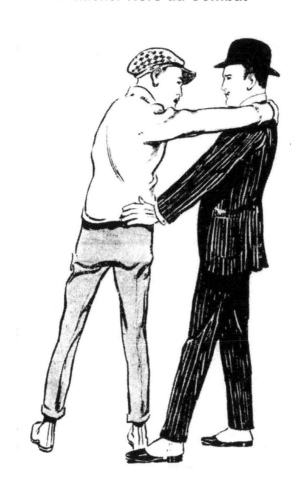

The illustrations which accompany this article show a trick which is easy to perform—and yet puts a thug at your mercy if you think quickly and act just as rapidly.

In the picture at the left the thug is shown in an effort to grab the intended victim around the throat. The "victim" as you will note, quickly places his left hand upon the thug's hip. Just as quickly he places his left leg behind the right leg of the thug and then, in lightning fashion, pushes his right hand under the thug's chin and pushes back the thug's head.

146

Meanwhile, he has shifted his left hand from the thug's hip to the small of the thug's back.

If you will look at the other illustration you will see the "victim" having the thug completely in his power. This is made possible only because the intended victim has placed his left leg **in back** of the right leg of the thug. If he hadn't done this the trick would be useless.

This trick can be cultivated very easily with a little practice.

> **Bob:** It's basically a chin jab. It has its place. If a guy is that close in range there are a number of things that could be done. A punch to the solar plexus is one. As Chris says stun and run!

> **Cris:** Yep, it's a variation on a chin jab. Now the question is, what do you do with him? Can't hold him in this position forever. As your left leg is behind his right leg, a quick sweeping motion will dump him on the ground, enabling you to walk away.

Tommy:

> Looks like a very awkward chin jab. It could be the illustration but seems very side on.

> This technique typically works best from the front, getting almost chest to chest.

Simple Grip That Holds Man Helpless

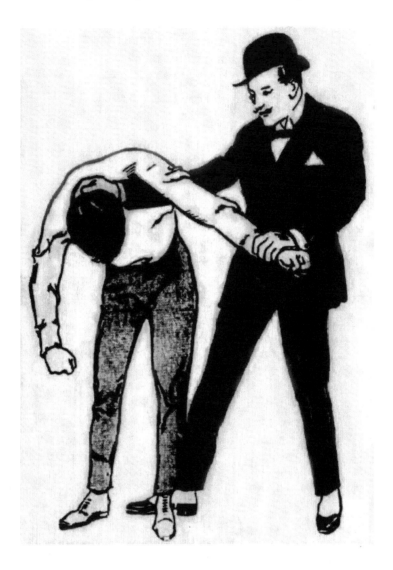

If you study the illustration which accompanies this article you will find how extremely simple it is for you to get a thug in your power by the use of a little speed and the trick which is illustrated.

In this particular instance the thug was about to grasp his intended victim. But the "victim" whirled quickly to the left side of the thug. He slipped his right foot back to the thug's left foot.

Having done so, he grabbed the left wrist of the thug, jerked his arm upward. And then the "victim" jammed his right arm under the thug's left and got a firm grip on the back of the thug's neck. And then, in completing the trick and in rendering the thug helpless, he simply pulled down the thug's left arm so that it rested against his forearm.

This trick is one of the most effective and one of the very best in subduing a thug. It all can be accomplished in the twinkling of an eye after it has been practiced and when you have the bully in the grip which is shown here he is absolutely helpless.

> **Cris:** Once again, what next? With your right foot behind his left foot, if you sweep out, he will land on his butt. Need to be careful of when you release the grip on the back of his neck, too soon and he can stand up and the sweep becomes more difficult, too late and you risk being dragged down with him. If the right foot is in front of the left leg, pressure on the neck can force a forward roll, similar to an aikido style throw.

> **Tommy:**
> I like this as an incidental, especially if I can dig my thumb into the jawbone, and then, when releasing, fire a punch right to that jaw.

> **Chris:** Standard armbar it looks like. I have a love-hate relationship with the arm bar. If done CORRECTLY, it's a very effective control technique with opportunities for takedowns and further control. The problem is, from what I have seen from lots of different instructors and systems is that it is rarely taught correctly and if applied the way it was taught, it would never work.

Splendid Exercise For Legs Is Bike Riding Without The Bike

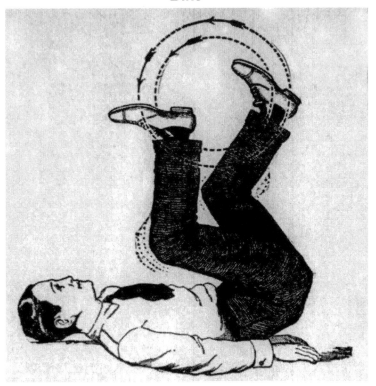

Inasmuch as sturdiness of legs is a mightily helpful fact in executing the tricks which will repel thugs, I am, in this article, showing a very simple but extremely effective form of exercise which will do wonders in developing leg as well as stomach muscles.

It is called the "riding the bicycle" exercise.

Lie on your back and raise your legs into the air. Place your hands on the floor alongside of your hips. Then move your legs in pedalling fashion— the same motion that you would go through if you were riding a bicycle.

Do the exercise before getting out of bed in the morning and after getting in bed at night. It is well not to go through these calisthenics when fully clothed. The fewer clothes the better, because that means free motion of the legs and a full play on the muscles of the legs and the stomach.

The first time you do this exercise you can pedal about fifty or sixty times, doing it easily. The next time cling to the same approximate number of "pedals" before increasing the motion.

Day after day you can increase the time devoted to this pedalling and also speed it up. After you have been doing it for a week or ten days you should be able to pedal at great speed for approximately two minutes, rest one minute, then pedal for two minutes, rest another minute and, in this way, put in ten full minutes of pedalling in the morning and ten minutes at night.

This form of exercise is a wonder not merely in strengthening the muscles of the legs and those of the stomach, but it also develops the lungs and will do wonders in toning up the intestinal tracts in the human body.

> **Cris:** Used to do this exercise in jiu jitsu and judo, also did circling exercises rotating from the knees.
>
> **Bob:** Not self-defense but.... This one I still do at the end of the abs conditioning portion of my boxing training. Coach always tells me to ride the bike. I never saw this being done outside of boxing. The lower you ride the bike with your legs, it works the lower portion of your abs. Strengthening the core. Stahara and all that.
>
> **Chris:** Sure why not, any ab exercise is good.

Variation Of Strangle Hold For One Who Dives For Your Legs

This article is accompanied by an illustration which shows a way that a thug can be repelled if he attempts to grab you by the legs.

In this particular picture the thug made a dive for legs of the intended victim. The "victim" grabbed his head, stuck his arms under the chin of the thug and pushed the head of the thug up against (the "victim's) stomach. The thug was then in his power.

Practice this trick and you will see how completely you can subdue a thug by such a hold.

Bob: The grovit is a nasty one. We trained this for a situation where a guy is rushing in to grab you.

It's definitely an effective and dangerous move. As usual I was concerned with how to extricate oneself from it. The answer was punch the guy in the nuts.

Cris: Bob calls it a grovit, I know it as a cross face. To add to the nastiness, place your left hand on the back of his shoulder, then form a figure 4 with your right hand on your left forearm.

Chris: I like this too. You can get the opponent in this position in a variety of ways, it doesn't have to just be a counter for a tackle. I do like how they mention grabbing the chin. I've done it both ways, with and without grabbing the chin and I feel you definitely get a stronger hold when you grab the chin.

Tommy:

A lovely technique. I tend to prefer this as a figure 4 crank on the neck, barring the face.

But even a twist like this when done with speed and power can be utterly devastating. A great move to consider if a grapple attack happens and there are more than one enemies to deal with.

Dempsey Tells How to Increase Power

Strength isn't a vital necessity for the performance of the tricks which I have outlined in this series of articles on how to repel thugs. But muscular power certainly would be mighty helpful in putting over these stunts.

Innasmuch as power in the hands, wrists and especially in the forearm is invaluable, I shall suggest several exercise which, if performed faithfully, should result in the generation of greater hand and arm power.

Here they are:

1. Extend hands straight out from the shoulder. Now close both fists slowly. When the fists are completely doubled and closed so tightly that you can't double them any more, hold them in that position for about ten seconds. Then open fists and relax muscles for a few seconds. Then repeat exercise. Do this about 20 times the first day you try it and increase it by five each day for about a week.

This exercise, if performed faithfully, will increase the muscular power within the hands, wrist and forearm in a wonderful way.

2. Open palm of left hand. Close fist of right hand. Place right fist into the palm of the left hand and try, with the fist, to push back the left hand. While the right hand is doing that, the left palm is to be used to resist the fist pressure. In other words, the fist pushes and the palm pushes back at it.

Hold to this battle between the palm and fist for about thirty seconds. Then stop and relax all the muscles. Now use the left fist to shove the right palm. Alternate in this way until you have pushed five times with each fist. That'll do for the first day.

The second day make it six or seven pushes for each fist. Increase the exercise until you are doing it about 25 times per day with each fist.

You'll be amazed by the improvement showing in the muscular power of the hands, wrists and forearms.

Dempsey Concludes List Of Self-Defense Series By Advocating Close Study

In concluding this series of articles on how to repel thugs I want to reiterate this vital points:

1. You must be sure always to retain a perfect balance when attempting any of these tricks.

2. They must be accomplished with all the speed that is possible. None of these tricks will be a success if it happens that you try them when you are off balance, or if you are so slow in attempting the execution that the thug can anticipate what you intend doing and thwart you before you can go through with your plan.

Throughout the series of articles I have included all forms of tricks to meet the ordinary emergency. I am sure that on or the other, used at the right time, can repel any attack which a thug intends to make. And as I have shown in these tricks. It is not necessary for you to be possessed of great muscular power. The presence of strength on your part will make it easier for you to put over the trick and put the thug at your mercy, but after all is said and done, the principal assets are to keep a perfect balance at all times and to act quickly.

There is always a likelihood that after a certain length of time has elapsed a person is likely to forget some of the trickeries which he had learned. That is probably in connection with the stunts which are outlined in my series of articles.

Therefore I would suggest that you save all the clippings and every few months that you perform the tricks all over again so as to reschool yourself until such time as the execution of the tricks is accomplished without the slightest hesitation on your part.

156

The Danish Kiss and some closing thoughts

This book became an experiment for me. It was sort of challenging initially to define the parameters for how I wanted this book to be. I knew I wanted to have some people weigh in from the group I host.

I wanted to get a good representation of people who train these type of techniques as well as some of the people who use them or teach them. I decided to let things develop on their own. The only ground rules were to provide commentary on the individual articles, pros and cons and perhaps what could be done better.

Regarding some of the techniques which may appear ridiculous, they might appear that way looking at them through our prism today. One has to remember that martial arts systems such as Judo and Jiujitsu didn't get fully introduced to the United States until after the second World War. During the 1920s, they were still somewhat of a novelty outside of military and law enforcement.

Looking at Dempsey, we see a famous boxer who could have easily flattened a thug out with one punch. With these articles, he didn't have years to train and teach the people reading them how to deliver a knockout. Instead, he tried to convey the best information he had available and put it into a user friendly format so that people might take away something useful. W. E. Fairbairn stated years later in *All-in Fighting* that "no-one will dispute the effectiveness of a straight left or a right hook to the jaw or body, but unfortunately it takes months of practice to develop a good punch."

Fairbairn was also dealing with time constraints when he developed his system to train commandos and spies during the war. Today we also look at some of the techniques as ridiculous or perhaps even useless; the "bronco kick" comes to mind.

Fairbairn put the techniques of his system into his wartime publications, attempting to convey similar information to civilians in the same way that Dempsey did in 1923.

Dempsey also later wrote a World War II-era manual on commando tactics. Jerry Powell pointed out to me that the text from the inside cover of *How To Fight Tough* states:

> In this book, Lieutenant Jack Dempsey not only teaches, but illustrates in pictures for which he himself posed, all the tricks he has employed in training men of the Coast Guard in the tough methods of Commandos.

> No American, man or woman, can predict when he or she might be called upon to engage—or, worse and more likely, to *meet*— the enemy in his or her home, his or her factory, or his or her main street.

It continues:

> *How to Fight Tough*, written by the toughest man in America, is a simple, clear, and complete illustrated textbook on how to deal with the enemy and subdue him-in any possible emergency. It is a handbook that no sensible American, in or out of the armed forces, can afford to be without. It covers the complete toughening up process taught by Lieutenant Dempsey to the men of the Coast Guard, big or small, man or woman, can master Lieutenant Dempsey's valuable tricks by carefully studying the book and practicing with friends.

The newspaper articles in 1923 were a precursor to Dempsey's hand-to-hand combat tactics book years later.

I thought it would be interesting to include an article from the 1940s to give an idea of what other boxers were thinking regarding non boxing defensive tactics which could be used against a thug.

In 1942 the sports columnist Tom O'Reilly wrote:

> Students of the Sweet Science, sunbathing on Jacobs Beach, felt slighted on hearing that the University of Illinois had appointed two physical educators to teach dirty fighting in a new course known as PEM-58.
>
> The PE stands for physical education, while the M signifies, not mayhem, but that the course is restricted to men. The teachers who plan to prepare students for army warfare, are Hek Kenney, wrestling coach and Herb Craig, fencing instructor.
>
> Jacos Beach critics remarked coldly, "Who'd them bums ever beat?"
>
> A poll, taken at full Gallup on 49th St., revealed that the most popular professors eligible for the Illinois Chair of Dirty Fighting included Tony Galento, Mickey Walker, Willie Lewis, Jack Dempsey, Gunboat Smith and—of all people—Tommy Loughran.
>
> It was pointed out that these men knew all about the Danish Kiss, Coney Island Triple, 10th Ave. Sneak and other adroit, if somewhat illegal gestures.
>
> The Danish Kiss is a street fighting maneuver that has been employed for years by Manhattan bartenders. Simply grab the victim by the coat lapels and pull him toward you. Then drop your forehead, which is the stoniest part of your skull, across the bridge

159

of his nose. It'll break the nose every time and also blacken both the victim's eyes.

Jack Dunstan, owner of the famous Jack's restaurant, is said to have accidentally given a Danish Kiss to Hype Igoe, a mild little man who kept his ukulele in Jacks' big ice box.

The Coney Island Triple consists of a kick in the shins, a knee in the groin and a Danish Kiss, all delivered in rapid succession. A man about to throw a 10th Ave. Sneak always argues while holding his suspenders or coat lapels with his fists. By gripping his clothing in this innocent fashion, he is in a perfect fighting pose and ready to throw either the right or left.

The ring's most common illegal maneuvers are butting, eye-gouging (with thumbs) elbow blows, the rabbit punch and the business of stepping with full force on an opponent's instep. Primo Carnera's feet were a menace and so are Fritzie Zivic's elbows.

Loughran was a beautiful boxer who didn't need to employ these methods, but ancients say he never missed any opportunities. The rabbit punch, which was not foreign to Jack Dempsey, was Gunboat Smith's prize weapon and, at the time, had a high-sounding title. It was called the Occipital Punch, because it consisted of hitting a man on the back of the neck at the point of his occipital bone.

The dirtiest fight ever staged? Tony Galento vs. Lou Nova was one. After flooring Nova Galento fell on him. Harry Greb vs. Mickey Walker was another. After battling at the Polo Grounds they met again for a two-hour brawl on 48th St. in front of the Silver Slipper. Mysterious Billy Smith bit off Joe Wolcott's ear.

And Kid McCoy reached the heights fighting a giant barefoot native in Capetown, Africa.

The Kid dropped some thumbtacks in the ring. When the native stepped on one and bent to pull it out, the Kid nailed him. Is there a doctor in the house?

I tried to do some further checking on the "Danish Kiss." I was able to locate an article in the Piedmont Journal, October 14th 1927 which mentioned the tactic in association with an ex-sailor named Franz Sowa. In Berlin on October 12th of that year, Sowa was captured. The article stated:

> After having evaded the police for several years, the ex-sailor Franz Sowa, a notorious footpad, wanted for felonious assault, blundered into the arms of the law by trespassing on the grass in a city park.
>
> When arrested for walking on the public green, Sowa, better known to the criminal fraternity as "Boxing Franz," at first gave his name as Soda. This strange appellation aroused the suspicion of the police, who, with his clue, succeeded in tracing his identity.
>
> "Boxing Franz" is famous among his pals for his two special methods of assault. One he calls the "Danish Kiss." It is a sharp blow with the edge of the flattened hand on the jugular vein, which causes the victim to drop senseless.
>
> The other, which he has artistically designated the "Liptrill," consists of a smashing blow of the fist on his victim's upper front teeth. While this later method does not always prove a knockout, it invariably renders the recipient powerless for a while.

At police headquarters "Boxing Franz" reproached himself for not having tried one or the other of his two infallible specialties on the police who arrested him.

The way Boxing Franz's technique is described, it sounds more similar to the edge of hand blow. Although Dempsey did not discuss what would become a signature technique during the second World War in his articles in 1927, he did discuss techniques which utilized the heel of hand blow. They would later appear prominently in many hand-to-hand combat texts during the war, notably in Fairbairn's works as the "chin jab."

In the Cumberland News, Saturday January 27th 1942, Dumb Dan Morgan, a famous boxing manager, described the heel of hand. He stated:

> The hardest thing to teach American soldiers is not to hit with the fists. The Marquis of Queensbury has done that to him. The heel of the hand is better. The knee is best.
>
> There is very pretty work [that] can be done with the knee and a punch with the *fists* is the lamest thing in the book, although it's the first thing our type guy thinks of when he gets mad. Sock him! All right sock him, but not with the fist I say. In a war they don't give you five or six rounds to wear your man down and set him up for a stiffener. If you don't win in one minute, you're dead the next minute."

Regarding Dempsey and the edge of hand blow, although he was probably already aware of the technique prior to the war, and although it did not appear in the articles in 1927, he later included it in his book.

In 1966 the Irish-American writer and former Welterweight Champion of the world Mushy Callahan, writing for the Irish Digest, made a mention of Dempsey and what he thought was the best blow in a street fight.

162

In an article titled *Can't Defend Yourself? What Nonsense!*, Callahan wrote:

> Whether a man is alone or with his wife or girlfriend he is sometimes threatened by thieves, pickpockets, queers, gangsters or just plain haters. The crime rate is on the increase the world over, and so is political murder and kidnapping.
>
> What can we do about it? Increase police protection? There aren't enough police to make the streets safe. That's been proven time and again. But we can learn to handle ourselves. And—surprise—in many cases it doesn't need Herculean strength.
>
> The theory is that when you are threatened you should just quietly give in and hand the thief whatever money or valuables you have. That doesn't always help. He is liable to use violence whether you accede to his demands or not. It's good to have an ace in the hole.
>
> For example, if a man threatens you from behind, you do not have to be his sitting-pigeon victim. What men forget is that the elbows are powerful weapons. A good right elbow whacked back into the solar plexus of the tormenter can often do the needed damage. It isn't necessary to get a judo hold on his neck or arm. If the hold goes wrong, you are in bodily contact and are in danger.
>
> I had sixty ring fights and, to the best of my knowledge, every one of them was clean. But in a street fight you *must* be dirty. When a threat is in front of you there is nothing more demoralizing to your attacker than a knee or foot to his groin. He'll fold up and await the police in writhing pain.

Some time ago a young girl stabbed a would-be attacker with a terminal blow and the victim of it is very likely to wish he were dead, instead of almost.

Jack Dempsey used to say he thought the best blow in a street fight if confronted with someone intent on burglary or worse is a backhand chop, which seems to come out of nowhere and for up-close effectiveness is unsurpassed.

Hitting an opponent in the neck or side of the head with a fast chop and connecting with the heel of the hand is a powerful counter.

Though I've never tried it outside the ring, sometimes in training and for a gag I'd step hard on the foot of my training partner. It would make him double up and hold his toes and then "whack" the finishing punch.

I've always though a fast stamp on an attacker's foot might do wonders, though I wouldn't recommend it until you've experimented with it.

When I asked for feedback on how the commenters felt the project was going I wanted to know if people still thought this book would be good enough to publish. Jerry Powell noted:

"I think it's a good way to keep the knowledge of dead and or dying systems alive. I also advocate as did many of the old homeland security self-defense, and early jiujitsu, karate, kung fu, boxing and wrestling courses that it was important to start your own club, assign club rank and just have fun with self-protection and learning life lessons."

Jerry then pointed out that Dempsey's book mentions the importance of learning the valuable tricks by carefully studying them and practicing them with friends. So if anything, that is what one should take away from this book. Take a handful of techniques. Train them constantly. Know them. Keep It Simple Stupid (K.I.S.S.).

In closing I will quote from an article that was posted on the Isshinkai Message List on September 18th 2003, in which my Hindiandi Kung Fu instructor's sensei, and former Marine hand-to-hand combat instructor, Arcenio James Advincula, wrote regarding K.I.S.S. Arsenio begins by discussing his sensei, the founder of isshin-ryu Karate, Tatsuo Shimabuku.

> Shimabuku said to learn all of the kata but master one and keep a few other techniques for fighting. Not the same as many think and the one thing I have been harping on. In a actual life and death situation, only the simplest tried and true techniques you are very familiar and have fine-tuned will have any success in working.

> The dojo is the laboratory where we can experiment and create different dojo bunkai. We can create a unlimited amount of techniques in a environment that is suited for the dojo or seminars, but for combat and in all reality, less is better. Dream, create and practice other bunkai but have a core foundation of kihon that you are comfortable with.

> Motobu is a prime example practicing mainly naihanchi shodan kata. Shimabuku always emphasized that it is not the number of kata but how well we knew a kata. We should all teach and learn all the kata and if one is trying to be an instructor it is mandatory you learn them all.

> It is a well-known fact that Chinto and Kusanku were Kyan's favorite kata. But these kata are suited for a small person who can use the double flying kicks and open hand techniques which

requires speed and flexibility. Shimabuku always talked about Kyan practicing Chinto kata on a bridge near his home.

As already stated each kata emphasizes different techniques better suited to different people. Each kata has its advantages. Remember what Nolan Webb said when he earlier this year visited with Tokumura on Okinawa, he said Tokumura said Sieunchin kata had everything in it for self-defense. In other words, this is probably Tokumura's main fighting kata. He has probably geared himself along with a few other basic techniques to use the various techniques found in seiunchin kata along with its strategy and tactics.

It is interesting that my Hindiandi instructor mainly taught me one kata with only a few techniques yet it is a formidable kata that is easy to use in a combat situation. Something like naihanchi and the way Motobu used the short kata.

If we look at the past history of kata, you will find that a kata was a fighting system or style in itself and was most likely created using techniques that its creator used successfully in actual encounters. Later the different masters started training with different teachers and learned other kata.

Today there are styles that have 50 or more kata yet if we look at Uechi-ryu originally they had only three kata. Today most would be bored practicing only kihon and one or two kata but in the past, this was the norm. People who understand will not practice 100 different techniques if they know they will really have to use it soon. They will practice only the techniques that they are comfortable with that are suited for their body type.

Since most of us will never have to use our skills if we follow our training to avoid conflict, it is good to learn and practice all our empty hand and kobudo kata. Variety is good and keeps us from getting bored. Looking for hidden techniques is good but in reality, nothing is better than block him and clock him, for it is the tried and true method passed down under the majority of Okinawan martial arts and they call it karate. As Shimabuku stated, Teach all kata but the most important is master one kata, along with a few other techniques.

Because a dragon hides in the clouds, we must remember, if every cloud had a hidden dragon, all they would do is get in the way. So sometimes seeing only the blue sky is good. Translation, KISS.

Despite all the karate terminology, my take away from that is: whether it is Dempsey's system, or Shepard's system, or one of the systems of Advincula's teachers, or any other system of self-defense out there, find someone who can teach it to you, find someone you can train it with, but train it and learn and understand the techniques. Like Bruce Lee said "Absorb what is useful. Discard what is not. Add what is uniquely your own." Also remember to just Keep It Simple Stupid.

Made in the USA
Las Vegas, NV
24 March 2023

69593867R00092